MARGARET THATCHER

The Woman Within

———————

MARGARET THATCHER

The Woman Within

Andrew Thomson

W H ALLEN · LONDON
1989

First published in 1989 by W H Allen & Co Plc,
Sekforde House, 175–179 St John Street, London EC1V 4LL

Edited by Moira Banks

British Library Cataloguing in Publication Data

Thomson, Andrew
  Margaret Thatcher: the woman within.
  1. Great Britain. Thatcher, Margaret
  I. Title
  941.085'7'0924

  ISBN 0 491 03429 6

Typeset by Phoenix Photosetting, Chatham, Kent
Printed and bound in Great Britain by
Mackays of Chatham PLC, Chatham, Kent

I dedicate this book, with love,
to another remarkable woman –
my mother, Agnes Woods Thomson

AUTHOR'S NOTE

The conversations and events in this book are based largely on my personal memories of the times I spent as a professional Conservative Party Agent.

During my years working as agent to Margaret Thatcher I realised that this book should be written. After retiring in 1987 and moving back to my native Scotland I realised that this book needed to be written. For the farther I go from Finchley, where she has been the Member of Parliament since 1959, the more I find she is misunderstood as a person and politician.

I confess that when she was first elected Leader of the Conservative Party in 1975, I did not think a woman was the right choice – I am on record as saying so. But like all who work with her and for her I became, and remain, one of her biggest fans.

Kelso, The Borders
January 1989

CONTENTS

BOOKS CONSULTED

Margaret Thatcher, Russell Lewis, Routledge and Kegan Paul, 1975
Margaret Thatcher, Patricia Murray, W H Allen, 1980
Margaret Thatcher, Wife, Mother, Politician, Penny Junor, Sidgwick
   and Jackson, 1983
Diary of an Election, Carol Thatcher, Sidgwick and Jackson, 1983

ACKNOWLEDGEMENTS

The author would like to thank the following for their kind
permission to reproduce the black-and-white photographs in this
book: Peter Beal, Rod Brewster and Jim Rowland of the *Hendon
and Finchley Times*; The Press Association; The Associated Press;
The Central Office of Information. He is also grateful to
Conservative Central Office for supplying copies of Mrs
Thatcher's speeches.

'She is multi-talented and multi-faceted yet the foundations of her belief are simple moral, economic and political truths.'

1

MEETING MARGARET THATCHER

A SMALL CUTTING from the satirical magazine *Private Eye* is still in my file. It states unequivocally that none of the Conservative Party's agents, and at that time in 1981 there were 275, wanted to be agent for Margaret Thatcher in her constituency of Finchley and Friern Barnet. Nothing could have been further from the truth. But then, so little of what is written about Margaret Thatcher is true. In fact, the post of agent in the Prime Minister's north London seat was highly attractive to some of my fellow agents. Many of them applied to Conservative Central Office in Westminster's Smith Square for the post. I was not among them. The rural life in Huntingdon was a pleasure for me, a Glaswegian brought up in that city's East End. There was no attraction in returning to a city, even the suburbs of north London. In addition, my work in Huntingdon was enjoyable enough, first looking after the somewhat crusty Sir David Renton as his career drew to a close as MP for the seat, then working with his young successor John Major.

The nearest I had ever come to thinking of working for a Prime Minister was the notion that John Major was more than just a candidate for swift promotion to the Cabinet. He had a sharp financial mind, a gentle easy-going manner, an excellent political instinct and the right background for a would-be leader these days

– the back streets of London's Lambeth. With his talents and the twin advantages of his working-class background and progress based on merit, he was clearly in the mould of the New Conservatives and a possible runner in a future leadership race.

It was a mark of the social changes wrought, largely by Margaret Thatcher, in the Conservative Party over the last twenty years that in the early 1980s a good working-class or lower-middle-class background was becoming desirable for aspiring leaders. The change was entirely to my liking, and meritocracy was a feature of Margaret Thatcher's values and politics that particularly appealed to me.

I had found my way into the Conservative Party via Glasgow's East End. There was little money; my father worked on the railways and my mother earned extra for the family by cleaning. But from early years I had a love of books and writing, generated, perhaps, by my father who brought home copies of *The Times* and *The Guardian* left in the carriages by the more wealthy passengers. My background was the penny library and a one-party socialist state which they call Glasgow, whose monopoly of power has been broken only once since 1933, and then for only a few short years by councillors called 'Progressives'. To call yourself Conservative in Glasgow was merely to encourage electoral disaster.

If ever there was a Thatcherite waiting for Thatcher, it was me. One part of me saw the failure of socialism in a home where in 1951–2 the rent was fifteen shillings a week while the rates were £2 – so that Glasgow could build the biggest council estate in Europe and then fill it with journalists, teachers and other professional people who could afford to buy their own homes but were being subsidised to encourage them to vote Labour. Another part of me saw horizons broadening beyond Glasgow, encouraged in part and probably unintentionally by my mother, who as a girl was a table maid to Lord Lovat at Beaufort Castle, Inverness. In later years, when I was five years old, she took me with her when she cleaned at the huge Glasgow tenement home of A. G. Barr who made Barr's Irn-Bru, a famous non-alcoholic drink that is popular even today. I was sat down in a chair and told: 'Sit still, Andrew.

[4]

Don't move.' But she allowed me to put the radio on so long as the station remained unchanged. To this day I cannot hear the BBC Third Programme, see polished floors or smell beeswax without thinking of the Scottish upper classes.

The Glasgow child grew up to spend the first years of his working life, until the age of twenty-seven, working in the fashion trade, and was always involved in the Conservative Party in Glasgow. In the late 1950s I was Vice-Chairman of the city's Young Conservatives and was asked by Sir Alick Buchanan-Smith, Chairman of the Conservative Party in Scotland, if I would consider becoming a full-time Party worker. In 1961 I was appointed Conservative Trade Unionist Organiser in Scotland, and in 1964 fought the Labour stronghold of Coatbridge and Airdrie as the Conservative Parliamentary candidate. Despite my high hopes the seat remained resolutely Labour, and I decided to concentrate on helping Conservatives win and hold their Parliamentary seats rather than try to get to Parliament myself.

So it came about that in October 1981, as the agent for Huntingdon, I walked up the steps of the Imperial Hotel in Blackpool, where the Conservatives were holding their third annual Party Conference since their 1979 election victory, for my first meeting with Margaret Thatcher. I have no idea to this day what thought processes within Conservative Central Office led senior figures there to contact me and say that my application was sought for the post of agent to Margaret Thatcher. Perhaps it was my reputation as an agent who would not behave as a political Yes Man; maybe that my political instincts were judged, correctly, to be gut Thatcherite.

Sir Anthony Garner, the Conservative Party's Director at that time, had suggested that we should meet at the Imperial. He greeted me in the hotel foyer. As we walked past security guards and met with no challenge, it became clear to me that the meeting was not to be confined to the two of us. We walked up the stairway, with Sir Anthony making the conversational point that Margaret Thatcher was really quite different from her image. That he found it necessary to make the point to one of the Party's agents is evidence enough of the fearful reputation she had in the land, as her position in the opinion polls and that of the Party plunged to one of their lowest ever points.

The scene that greeted me inside the Prime Minister's suite was not one that a man born and bred in Glasgow would have expected. The lady was mixing the drinks. Where I was reared it was always the men who took charge of this duty. (In the years to come it became almost natural to see Margaret Thatcher insisting on performing this role, no matter who were her guests. She would line up with almost fanatical precision the bottles of tonic beside the gin, and the ginger ales beside the whisky.) She said: 'I understand that you want to be my agent.' It was not an occasion for indecision. I said 'Yes. I'm coming to London.' My decision was made spontaneously as I spoke.

The journey back to Huntingdon after the Party Conference left me slightly dazed at what I had done. Subject to the formal approval of me by the Finchley Conservative Association, I had decided to return to the city life which I disliked and become Margaret Thatcher's agent. I was also puzzled by my brief encounter with the bustling woman with the drinks and easy manner. She had none of the presence of other Conservative Party Leaders I had met, no trace of the bearing, manner or profundity of Harold Macmillan, Sir Alec Douglas Home or even Edward Heath. But clearly there had to be a special quality in her to have become Britain's first woman Prime Minister and, in the absence of any substantial successes to her credit over those first eighteen months, to be digging into power with such resolution.

Over my subsequent six years with her, the question of what this special quality is nagged at me, just as it had on the car drive back to Huntingdon. It was a question that would be asked throughout Europe, North America and eventually even in the Soviet Union as Britain left behind what had seemed to be a never-ending downward spiral of economic decline. The longer the recovery of the British economy, the more apparent the self-esteem and confidence of its people, the more clear it became to our friends and allies – and also to those not quite so well disposed towards us –

that it was all connected with Margaret Thatcher and the qualities she took with her to 10 Downing Street. Over and over again I asked and was asked, 'What is the secret?'

As I began to know her, the best way to define her seemed more and more as 'ordinary'. Of course, she has not survived and prospered as Party Leader and Prime Minister simply because of her ordinariness. She has many extraordinary abilities, but none of them is a definition in itself of the real Margaret Thatcher. She is a very simple, ordinary lady with a gift for understanding the essential qualities and ambitions of the British people. But, like many women, she likes to maintain a little mystery and paradox about herself. So she will change her mind at the last minute, take spur-of-the-moment decisions, or insist on seeing someone whom she said an hour earlier she would not. But these are the mere decorations of daily life, and on the important issues of loyalty and political and economic principles she does not change her mind.

An aide who became personally very close to the Prime Minister was asked if she understood her. 'I become convinced that I understand her,' came the response, 'and then she does something that proves I don't really understand her at all.' I am sure as you read this book you will find the same dilemma. But on the bread-and-butter issues of political and economic life, the aide knew exactly where Margaret Thatcher stands and has stood unwaveringly since she went up to Oxford from the grocer's shop in Grantham. She is multi-talented and multi-faceted yet the foundations of her belief are simple moral, economic and political truths. Unlike so many other people who are intelligent and well-educated, she does not seek out the complexities of politics and economics, or delight, like so many intellectuals, in making a puzzle out of a simple truth. On the contrary – she delights in reducing complexities to essential truths.

She has been simultaneously loved and reviled within her own country probably more than any Prime Minister this century, and has secured as great a stature on the international stage as Winston Churchill. It is improbable that the Conservative MPs who pushed her into challenging Edward Heath for the leadership in 1975 saw in her the secrets of success that I was to seek to define. Equally, it is unlikely that in 1940 the backers of Churchill saw in him the secret to our wartime salvation. Winston Churchill and Margaret Thatcher were the best to hand against what seemed hopeless odds. In 1940 we either capitulated or fought what looked like an unwinnable war. In 1975 we either capitulated to trade-union rule, corporatism and the seductive slide into hyper-inflation and banana-republic politics, or the Conservative Party started to fight to restore some basic truths which most of its MPs at Westminster seemed to have long forgotten.

Before her third successive General Election victory, it made many Conservatives not a little uncomfortable to liken Margaret Thatcher to Churchill. The comparison could and should have been made much earlier, not for their style of leadership but because each was motivated in the final analysis by a simple faith in the British people. Margaret Thatcher actually believes in de Toqueville's analysis of British greatness: that for an explanation you look not to our coal, ores and minerals, nor to our forests and seas, but to the people themselves. She believed that all that was needed was to set the people free – to decide for themselves whether to go on strike, to decide for themselves whether to join a union, to buy the council home they lived in, to invest their savings abroad, to send their children to the school that seemed to offer the best for them.

The concept was remarkably simple. In 1981 when we met in Blackpool, it was only the implementation that was so difficult. Most of her Cabinet thought the idea either impossible or undesirable, and the opinion polls indicated that the British people in whom she had such faith did not, perhaps, hold quite the same faith in her.

As I started work for her as her agent in Finchley and Friern Barnet, I began to see how the gradual transformation of Britain was wrought by the vision and vigour of one woman. But what motivates her and makes her what she is cannot be found in the dry background details of her life. As Margaret Roberts, a grammar-school girl, she went up to Somerville College, Oxford where she got an Upper Second. She went on to become a research chemist from 1947 until 1951 when she married Denis Thatcher. They subsequently had twins, Carol and Mark. While bringing them up as toddlers she took a law degree, then won Finchley for the Conservatives in 1959, became Leader of the Opposition in 1975 and Prime Minister in 1979. That tells you everything about Margaret Thatcher – and yet it tells you nothing about her as a person.

It soon became clear to me that the real Margaret Thatcher had been distorted in the reflections of the media and by the managers of her public image. She can be ruthless. She can weep. She is much more than the product of her starched biographical résumé. She is a woman, a mother, above all a patriot and Britain's first female Prime Minister. She remains, despite the years of publicity and power since 1979, largely misunderstood. Her name and her photograph are enough to excite adulation or hatred; people are rarely indifferent to her. So powerful have the very name and media image become that few people today seem even to consider that there are many other faces to Margaret Thatcher. On the important issues she may be ordinary and populist, but the many other facets of her character and personality were to become rapidly clear to me after I joined the Member of Parliament for Finchley and Friern Barnet as her agent.

'If Margaret Thatcher had a motto on her desk, it would read "No Cheques Accepted".' (Paul Johnson)

2

HOUSEWIFE AND GROCER'S DAUGHTER IN NUMBER 10

MARGARET HILDA ROBERTS was born in Grantham on 13 October 1925. Sixty years later, the legacy of her childhood as a grocer's daughter and her experience as a housewife and mother still dominate her thinking, both in 10 Downing Street and in her dealings with everyone she meets, from President Reagan to the ordinary people who visit her at the Finchley Conservative Association's offices. It became a denigrating jibe after her election as Conservative Leader that she was a grocer's daughter. Paternalists in the Party who believed that they had a birthright to shape its thinking would sneer at her 'corner-shop values'. In fact, corner-shop values have never been alien to most members of Conservative Associations, but by the 1970s most seemed increasingly shamefaced about them. It was the articulation of these values by Margaret Thatcher that seemed so extraordinary in those early days – they were beliefs that were generally held in the Associations, but not something that decent people thought they could talk about in public. She argued that running a country should be like running that corner shop, or like a housewife running the family budget.

As long ago as September 1949, when she was Prospective Conservative Candidate for Dartford, where she cut her political teeth before moving on to the safer Finchley and Friern Barnet seat, she told a Ladies' Luncheon Club in Edward Heath's neighbouring constituency in Bexley, Kent: 'Don't be scared of the high-flown language of economists and Cabinet Ministers, but think of politics at our own household level. After all, women live in contact with food supplies, housing shortages and the ever-decreasing opportunities for children, and we must therefore face up to the position, remembering that as more power is taken away from the people, so there is less responsibility for us to assume.'

In these two sentences, uttered almost forty years before she became the longest-serving Prime Minister of the century, is the essence of Thatcherism. Her central economic philosophy is simple. The struggle that she had in her first years in 10 Downing Street in getting her Cabinet colleagues to accept those simple truths belies the facts of today, when they have become in large measure the norm for the major political parties in the United Kingdom and, as a philosophy, have become one of our biggest exports. The second part of the extract from her 1949 speech was the forerunner to the sale of council homes, the selling of the nationalised industries, and giving people more choice in the education and health services. She does not trust politicians at national or local level, preferring to see power in the hands of the people. In all her off-the-cuff remarks and conversations in Finchley, this truth recurs time and again.

Her father stood 6 feet 2 inches tall and was a grocer who had left school at the age of twelve. Her mother was a dressmaker. One grandfather was a shoemaker, the other a railway guard (as was my father). In the family flat over the shop on the busy crossroads in what has been called the 'slum' end of town, there was no bath and no hot water. Baths were once a week with hot water carried to the tub in the wash-house at the back of the shop. It was in that flat that Margaret Hilda Roberts was born, two years after her sister, Muriel, and where their upbringing was, according to one friend's reported account, 'never rich, never poor'. But what the Roberts lacked in riches was made up in values instilled by Alfred Roberts, the Methodist, Rotarian, local Alderman and father of Margaret, whose influence on her today is at times highly evident.

He is said to have been the best-read man in Grantham and his second daughter, Margaret, had an adoration for him that has never faltered. Every week she collected books for him from the library, his special interests being current affairs and the Welfare State. He did not drink alcohol and was a stalwart of the local community who, when he was not managing the grocer's shop, was active either in the local Chamber of Trade or on the council. He believed in service to the community as well as more directly to his customers, and it is from him that Margaret Thatcher learned her abiding principles in life and in politics. The strict Methodist convictions of Alfred Roberts were buttressed in the home by Margaret's maternal grandmother, who was filled with the Victorian values that her grand-daughter was to espouse later in 10 Downing Street. She lived with the family for ten years after her daughter Beatrice and son-in-law Alfred pooled their savings during the First World War to buy the shop on North Parade.

Some of Margaret Roberts' most formative years with her father before she set off from Kesteven and Grantham Girls' School were the years of the Second World War, gloomy and unexciting days in that provincial English market town. There were no bright lights, glamour or distractions: nothing to take her out of the flat above the shop, and every incentive to stay there, reading like her father and becoming very much like him in so many other ways. Bespectacled and with a huge mop of blond hair, Alfred Roberts insisted that the family follow him four times on a Sunday, their only day off from the shop, to the Finkin Street Methodist Church. He saw that his daughter was taught first to play the piano, at which she was by all accounts very gifted, and then to speak without a Lincolnshire accent – he sent her to elocution lessons just before she went up to Oxford.

Just how much of an influence Alfred Roberts was on her, in contrast to her mother, can be gauged from Margaret Thatcher's entry in *Who's Who*, written, as are all such entries, by the subject. The standard form is for the subject to name both father and mother. Margaret Thatcher's entry states baldly that she is daughter of the late Alfred Roberts, Grantham, Lincolnshire. Her mother is not mentioned, and whatever else her ten-line entry shows, it demonstrates the extent to which her father lives on in her today.

Margaret's mother seems to have been very much a secondary figure, a housewife, mother and washer and polisher of the linoleum floors in the Roberts' home where, as Margaret Thatcher has remarked, cleanliness was next to godliness, in part at least because of the rules laid down by her Victorian grandmother. Beatrice Roberts seems to have been the reverse of her daughter in some ways. She was quite, plain, dressed without inspiration and wore her hair in a bun. But she taught her daughter to bake bread, and Margaret remains to this day an accomplished cook. Beatrice, a deft seamstress who made the children's clothes, also taught her to sew and make dresses, skills which she has not only retained but still uses. Even today, when Margaret Thatcher buys curtains she insists on big hems so that she can let them down if necessary when she moves on.

She has said of her mother: 'I loved her dearly, but after I was fifteen we had nothing more to say to each other. It wasn't her fault. She was weighed down by the home, always being in the home.' Instead, the teenage Margaret looked to her father. To this day, she is still trying to live up to his expectations; she confides to friends even now that her father would say that he expected 'great things' of his daughter Margaret. She learned one priceless lesson at Alfred's feet: to think for herself and not to follow unquestioningly the thoughts of others. This, as much as the grocer's-shop economics, is responsible for today's Prime Minister.

Always bright beyond her years as a child, she studied in a form above her age. But she was never brilliant. Her successes stemmed from great efforts, not the easy genius of some scholastic stars. She seems to have been good at games, too. She played for the school hockey team in the position of centre-half – an interesting position for a future politician to be in, because it is from that spot that the game is controlled. At the age of ten, a year younger than was normal, she passed a scholarship examination for Kesteven and Grantham Girls' Grammar School where in the succeeding seven years she failed to come top only once. Margaret Roberts appears to have been one of those children who in any age infuriate their contemporaries. She was good at everything, including games and drama. It is no surprise that Gladys Foster, a former school friend, is recorded as recalling: 'Mothers would say to their daughters: "Why can't you be more like Margaret?"'

She was fired from an early age with the idea of becoming an MP and is said to have begun discussing the ambition with friends at school from the age of thirteen or fourteen. It was perhaps for this reason that she had an inclination to debate, manifested in her performances in the school debating club. Local politicians were always in and out of the grocer's shop and the flat as part of the life of Alderman Roberts. She later told schoolchildren in Finchley: 'We always talked about politics at home.' She was still a teenager and not long up at Oxford when the 1945 General Election was called, but she was sufficiently advanced as a politician to be the warm-up turn at Conservative election meetings in Grantham before the major speaker, either the candidate or a visiting senior Conservative, stood up to speak.

She saw Oxford as the best way of furthering her ambition to become an MP. Her determination to get to Oxford is recalled by those who remember her in those days, and her route to the university, which was then much harder for girls to reach, was typically calculated. She decided that she stood the best chance with chemistry, and was urged by Miss Dorothy Gilles, her plain-speaking Scottish headmistress, to wait until her third year before sitting her Oxford entrance examination. Margaret was too young at seventeen, claimed the headmistress, to go to Somerville College. The suggested delay left Margaret Thatcher infuriated. In fact she got to Oxford when she wanted, but the intervention of Miss Gilles left her forever resentful. Upon returning to the school years later, she apparently corrected Miss Gilles in public. That was a precursor of the Margaret Thatcher of 10 Downing Street. She does not forget those who seek to thwart her.

It may be too simplistic to portray the Margaret Roberts who arrived at Somerville College as having political views taken straight from her father. His politics seem to have been shaded more towards the Liberal Party than the Conservatives, and by the time she reached university his daughter had taken his counsel and begun to think everything through for herself. He joined Grantham Council as an Independent two years after his younger daughter was born and served as Chairman of the Finance Committee as well as Mayor. He was effectively 'sacked' from the council in 1952 by the Labour group, who claimed back his aldermanic seat. When Margaret Thatcher recounts his words after his removal from the council, she is prone to tears. He said: 'No medals, no honours, but an inward sense of satisfaction. May God bless Grantham forever.' With those words, he laid down his aldermanic robes.

So the Margaret Roberts who arrived at Oxford may not have been a political clone of Alfred Roberts. But she was, and is remembered as being, totally Conservative from her first day and impervious for the following four years (her chemistry degree required an additional year on top of the usual three) to all arguments that were non-Conservative. Of course, the brand of Conservatism that was to become Thatcherism does contain some elements of the old Liberalism, notably a passion for free trade and an attachment to laissez-faire economics. Just what brand of Conservatism she espoused at Oxford in 1943 is not recorded, but the collective memory of fellow undergraduates of the time is that she arrived a Conservative, left a Conservative and never for a moment in between considered being anything else.

It has been suggested that her Oxford days saw something of a snob emerge in Margaret Roberts, that she wanted to know only those who could advance her political ambitions and that she turned her back on Grantham, not returning to the middle-England town because she was clearly on her way to Westminster. I do not know whether there is any truth in all this. But I do know that she is not a snob now, believing, rather, that the intellectual socialists are the real snobs. She is fond of saying that they think they have talent and ability that none of the rest of the human race possesses. 'That is the ultimate snobbery,' she says, 'the worst form of snobbery there is. Only put them in charge and the poor will have everything. So the poor put them in power and discover that the rulers have everything and the poor have nothing.'

What I do know is that if she did try to put Grantham behind her during and immediately after her Oxford years, she failed, as she was bound to do. We are all the products of our childhoods. In the case of Margaret Roberts, her middle-class, Methodist background spawned a bristling meritocrat, an individual who does not believe in luck or personal favours, but who believes in rewards in return for endeavours. There is a story that, at primary school, she won a poetry-reading prize at a local drama festival and her headmistress said, 'You were lucky Margaret!' The headmistress must have been among the first to regret the ill-judged word uttered in front of the then Margaret Roberts, because she replied: 'I wasn't lucky. I deserved it.' The element of luck simply does not enter into her equations – not surprisingly for someone who was both born and married on the supposedly 'unlucky' thirteenth. The achievements she made – Oxford, Westminster, 10 Downing Street – were secured because of her efforts, and these in turn were founded on her father's ambitions for her.

After almost a decade living above a more famous establishment in Downing Street, Margaret Thatcher never tires of delivering homilies based on her experiences as a child in the Grantham shop. These experiences do not have to be dredged from her memory; for her, they are lessons of life as valid today as they were in the 1930s, when she would stand behind the shop counter. A principle learned in those days is described in her own words: 'As a young girl standing behind the counter, the first thing I was taught to say was "Can I help you?"' Another favourite is that people must be 'given their weight' – a reference to the rule in the grocer's shop that customers got exactly the amount they were paying for. She will often draw, too, on her father's rule that customers 'don't have credit'.

Her father's exhortation that customers should be 'given their weight' lives on in her at all times, as colleagues who went with her to America recall fondly. She was a guest at a Republican 'plate' dinner in America with George Bush, an occasion when the guests pay a large sum of money for the privilege of attending, to boost party funds. This was a vast dinner and afterwards guests and other onlookers pushed towards the American politicians and Margaret Thatcher to get a closer look, or even to exchange a sentence or two. Faced by the advancing horde, the Republicans made for a tunnel exit. Margaret walked towards the advancing crowd, explaining: 'Do you know how much people paid to come here? Five hundred dollars! We must give them value for money.'

It is the spirit of that Grantham of the 1930s that permeates her fundamental beliefs in how Britain as a whole – and the individual families within it – used to behave and should behave today. It was this quintessential Margaret Hilda Roberts who spoke to Conservatives in 1982 about the responsibilities of the individual in the old days, with the emphasis on maintaining this code of conduct today.

> You worked hard because that was what life was about, and you paid your way.
>
> You did not have what you could not pay for.
>
> You kept your word and you settled your debts.
>
> You were taught to be polite, because it made life more agreeable and tolerant.
>
> You declared your earnings honestly and paid your taxes dutifully, because it was right.
>
> You lived below your earning power in order to save, to put something by.
>
> Morality was strict by the standards of the permissive society, perhaps even stuffy by any standards, but better than no morality at all.
>
> You supported the police and disapproved of violent crime.

Alderman Roberts' admonition 'Never be in anyone's debt' is a maxim by which she lives in all her own personal dealings. At a pre-Christmas fair in Finchley she saw a display of photographs of herself which had appeared in a local newspaper. She expressed regret that she had never been an amateur photographer and, as if intent on compensating in one day for the omission of an entire lifetime, she began ordering photographs from the startled photographer, Graham Greaves. Some days later he received a phone call from 10 Downing Street. Joy Robilliard, the Prime Minister's constituency secretary, explained that having ordered the photographs, Margaret Thatcher wanted to know how much money she should send. Graham responded that it was privilege enough that the Prime Minister wanted his photographs. It was not just politeness on his part; he meant it. Joy Robilliard relayed the reply to the Prime Minister, who insisted that the photographer must be phoned again. For three months, the phone calls from Joy continued as the Prime Minister demanded the bill. Finally, at another Conservative Association function in Finchley one Friday evening in the subsequent spring, Margaret caught sight of Graham Greaves, hurried across the room to take his arm and insisted: 'Young man, I owe you money.'

This near-obsession with personal debt is a constant source of complications for those around her, such as Joy Robilliard, who has worked with Margaret Thatcher since she went to 10 Downing Street and who is now so close to her that at times she has a sixth sense for sticky situations. In March 1987 when Margaret Thatcher set off to open a new Sainsbury's store in North London, Joy's warning to all was that whatever happened the Prime Minister must not be permitted to stop anywhere in the shop. She must at all costs be kept moving at a brisk walk, otherwise she would begin shopping. If that happened, warned Joy, the day's tightly programmed schedule would fall apart.

Her instructions were heeded. The Prime Minister entered Sainsbury's at something not much short of a gallop which was maintained until she, the store executives and party aides began to pass the meat counter. 'Hold on,' cried the Prime Minister, 'I need meat for the weekend.' She bought three pounds of mince for a shepherd's pie for Denis, then discovered that she had no money in her handbag and told the meat-counter manager to send her the bill. For months afterwards Joy Robilliard could not meet the Prime Minister without facing a demand to know whether the mince bill had been paid. Explanations that Sainsbury's regarded three pounds of mince as a keepsake were rebuffed. She was insistent. Suggestions that the cost of providing the account would exceed the cost of the mince failed to budge her. Flouting Alderman Roberts' principle on debt affronted her.

The greater the pressures upon her, the more she will fall back on the simple truths of her childhood. So in 1981, when the pressure for an economic U-turn was at its most intense and no less than 364 economists got together to sign a letter published in *The Times* stating that she was wrong, it was the grocer's daughter who responded to them in a speech to the Scottish Conservatives' annual conference in Perth. 'Having myself been brought up over the shop, I sometimes wonder whether they back their own forecasts with their money,' she said. It was a well-aimed dig at what she called 'the 364 academic pessimists'. For outside of the universities – out in the real world– investors were beginning to put their money on Margaret Thatcher, and the stock market was beginning to climb.

It was again the grocer's daughter and housewife who spoke out to the Conservatives at Bournemouth in March 1980 on the need for cash limits throughout Whitehall to curb its spending. 'All of us have cash limits,' she exclaimed with a hint of exasperation. 'Every family, every independent company, every corner shop faces the same blunt truth: cash is limited. They don't have a right, the company doesn't have a right, to come and get extra money from the Government if they mismanage their affairs. Why should a nationalised industry be different?'

Her priority of making inflation the number one economic enemy stems in large measure from those Grantham days. Before she took power in 1979, there were mounting problems in four key economic areas: unemployment, sterling, the balance of payments and inflation. Before she arrived at Number 10, economists, politicians and academics seemed agreed that the trick was to get all four in balance simultaneously. Margaret Thatcher set the conquering of inflation as her priority, constantly referring to the pensioners who watched their savings being ruthlessly destroyed by the erosion of the currency. Her speeches from those days are littered with the plight of the elderly, whom she sees as if they were her parents or her constituency pensioners: hard-working, thrifty, prudent in their early and middle years, carefully saving the pennies and pounds for the comfort of their old age and to have enough to pay for a funeral. Saving for the rainy day was something drilled into the young Margaret Roberts in the flat over the grocer's shop from which she would walk each week to the post office to buy her National Savings stamps. The duty of the State in Margaret Thatcher's eyes is not so much to provide for the old who were feckless in their younger days, but to ensure that the provision which the more prudent have made for themselves is protected from inflation so that it retains its value.

In 1974, after the announcement that she would challenge Edward Heath for the Party Leadership, she was plunged almost immediately into a storm over an interview with a magazine for pensioners called *Pre-retirement Choice*, in which she suggested that the elderly should keep a store of tinned food as a safeguard against the inflationary whirlwind being unleashed by the Labour Government's policies. It was a harmless enough remark, but was immediately interpreted in some quarters as evidence of greed on her part. A leading member of the Consumer Association expressed her 'disgust' at the 'hoarding' proposed by Margaret Thatcher. She said: 'It is just for greed. Only the rich can afford to hoard food or have enough space to stock-pile.' When the row spread to the Commons, Margaret Thatcher retorted that what she had recommended was simply sensible buying for a housewife when the pound in her purse was shrinking. The advice could have come straight from Alderman Roberts, who would have recommended that if the value of your money is falling fast, then the best thing you can put it into is a stock of groceries.

It might have been expected that since she has lived in Number 10 since 1979 with a husband who is reputed to be a millionaire, the value-for-money theme might have been diluted a little in her personal life, if not in her Government. Not a bit of it. Though her personal finances and those of Denis Thatcher are more than adequate, even by the standards of the well-off, she still buys toilet rolls in bulk in Finchley for the flat over Number 10 and for their home in Dulwich.

She exercises the same carefulness when wrapping Christmas presents. All her gift tags are hand made, carefully cut from previous years' Christmas cards. She may, of course, have bought the do-it-yourself tags at local fêtes to raise money for Conservative funds. But a Prime Minister who is as careful as Margaret Thatcher is with the pennies – those in her own pocket as well as those of the taxpayer – may well make time at Chequers in the autumn weekend evenings to make her own gift tags from last year's cards.

Margaret Thatcher's attitude to the spending of taxpayers' money is summed up by her oft-repeated remark to constituents: 'I always treat other people's money as if it were my own.' In turn, the way she treats her own money was best described in her own words when she attended a reception at a Finchley bank. In order to assist the photographers with their job of trying to find an original picture of her, she was asked to try out the bank's cash machine. She looked at it with a mixture of puzzlement and fear and then confessed that she had never actually used one before, although Denis did. Of course, it could be argued that a Prime Minister would never need to use a cash machine at a bank, but she added a revealing explanation. 'I have always been fearful that someone might be watching and snatch the money,' she told her hosts.

For a Government that has presided at times over huge expansions in personal credit, she has more than an antipathy towards it in her personal life. She destroyed her own credit card when her bank wrote telling her that her credit limit had been raised without her requesting it. In addition, there are at least three bank executives of relatively humble status who know exactly how she feels about the offering of bank credit to people little over eighteen years old. She spotted the bank managers in December 1987 at the Westminster Finchley Forum in her constituency, a dining group

Mr and Mrs Denis Thatcher

The new Member of Parliament for Finchley with twins Carol and Mark in 1959

An English Rose

The 'Old Girl' back at school in Grantham

Shopping is a serious business for the grocer's daughter

The happy couple 'at home' at the Finchley Association Dinner Dance

The Thatcher Family meets the Finchley Family on Polling Day

Mr and Mrs Mark Thatcher

'A woman's work is never done'

designed to keep her in touch with local businessmen. They were huddled quietly in a corner with their glasses of wine until she cut a swathe through the throng to accost them. Why, she demanded, were they lending so much money to students? What, she asked, were the banks doing about credit cards for students? Did the banks actually know what they were doing? The bank officials were clearly not at the level where responsibility lay, as the sheer frozen look in their eyes underlined. Though they did not realise it at the time, they had just become honorary members of that group of people, mostly Conservative Ministers, who have been 'handbagged' by the Prime Minister. She looms into view with her handbag swinging with dangerous vigour, and leaves her victims feeling as if she has swung it in a mighty blow across the temple.

Margaret Thatcher's father taught her more than simple economics. Her caution in reforming the National Health Service and the social security system has surprised some of her right-wing supporters. But she is not a right-wing ideologue with narrow vision. As she remarked after the 1987 General Election: 'In the hearts of the people they want those who are genuinely unfortunate to be looked after. Never fear that I don't understand. Those are the fundamentals I learned from my father.'

For those in the Government who disagree with her politics, the influence of her father can be alarming. There is one particular maxim of his which she still quotes:

It is easy to be a starter
But are you a sticker too?
It is easy enough to begin a job
It is harder to see it through.

This forms the basis of one of Margaret Thatcher's most remembered lines from her speeches. In her end-of-Party Conference peroration in October 1980, at a point when her Government was sinking to its lowest point, with newspapers and television expecting, almost willing her to change the economic course, she said: 'To those waiting with bated breath for that favourite media catchphrase, the U-turn, I have only one thing to say: "You turn if you want to. The lady's not for turning."'

No one who knew Alderman Roberts would have been surprised by that speech and her determination. After all, on winning her first General Election she had paid this tribute to him: 'He brought me up to believe all the things I do believe and they are the values on which I have fought the election. It is passionately interesting to me that the things I learned in a small town, in a very modest home, are just the things that I believe have won the election. I owe almost everything to my father.'

'Arthur Scargill and the strike – we are doing the right thing?'   (Margaret Thatcher)

3

BEHIND THE IRON LADY'S MASK

IN A SPEECH two months after she won power, Margaret Thatcher set out in detail her views on the legacy she had inherited from the Labour Government. It was a real 'Iron Lady' speech which I recalled well when I joined her as agent, but it did nothing to prepare me for the surprise of the woman behind that image. The speech concentrated on the 'irresponsibility and inhumanity' of the Winter of Discontent and trade-union anarchy permitted by the outgoing Labour Government; the 'wanton expansion' of the State's powers and a consequent 'great drop in public spirit'; a 'great private discontent' bred of excessive public spending; the undermining of private philanthropy and voluntary organisations; a heavy tax burden that had lowered fiscal morality with the growth of the 'malignant cancer' of the black economy; a loss of moral standards and with it the idea of doing any bit of work as well as it could be done. The speech told me everything about her as a politician – and nothing about her as a person.

Against the backdrop of that and similar speeches, she launched into her political programme with the zeal of the conviction politician and the image, at home and abroad, of the Iron Lady. That image was right for the times. I do not seek to underplay the un-yielding aspects in her character; she can be dogmatic, singleminded and very tough. But there is also a sense of uncertainty within her which is never glimpsed behind the Iron Lady image. It is an uncertainty that can strike at her very political soul, as happened one night in November 1984 during the final months of the miners' strike. She was sitting at her desk in the Finchley Conservative Association's headquarters at 212 Ballards Lane, signing some of her hundreds of Christmas cards, when she looked up, her pen frozen in her hand, and asked: 'We *have* got it right, haven't we?' For a moment, there was no indication as to what she was talking about. Then she explained: 'Arthur Scargill and the strike – we *are* doing the right thing?'

On the coalfields the National Union of Mineworkers pickets were convinced that Margaret Thatcher was committed blindly and without hesitation or reservation to breaking Arthur Scargill, the President of their union, and their strike. It was not that the Prime Minister that night was seeking *my* opinion on the correctness or otherwise of what was not so much the Cabinet's strategy as her strategy. Her question was addressed as much to the pictures of herself on the walls as to me. It was as though a doubt had surfaced in her consciousness during the continuous reflex action of signing her Christmas cards at the desk. I was as surprised as a picket from the NUM would have been. But she clearly needed reassurance, so I reminded her that the majority of the people in Britain supported her, how members of the NUM were being intimidated, and of the bravery of the miners in the breakaway Union of Democratic Mineworkers. My words were nothing more than she would have got from the average man in the local pub, but they were enough for the Prime Minister to begin to pick up my thread, to reflect on the courage of the men in the UDM and of the need not to let them down, and to remember that Governments cannot do everything for everyone.

The moment of uncertainty and self-doubt had passed, but it left behind the impression of a woman very different to that painted by the Downing Street public relations machine.

On the major issues of politics and economics her beliefs are unchanging, but they are edged with caution, uncertainty and at

[30]

times just a little self-doubt which are never displayed in public and rarely even among those who work closest to her. Even on that most fundamental of issues, the running of the economy, she confessed after the 1987 General Election that she had harboured some doubts that her policies would work in the early days. It was not that she did not believe in the correctness of the policies or in the wisdom of freeing up the economy. Her anxiety was that after years of Labour rule the British workers, when given their freedom, might not respond immediately with greater productivity. She feared, as she wondered aloud in a post-election interview with Brian Walden in the *Sunday Times*, that the years of socialism might have blunted the edge of the British people, so that they would not respond spontaneously to the new freedoms. As events have shown, she was wrong to have harboured these doubts, but clearly on this economic issue, as on the major trade-union and industrial issues to confront her Government, she had wondered at times: 'Are we doing the right thing?'

The great issues of State aside, Margaret Thatcher can be a contrary individual. But, as she is Prime Minister, her contrariness is felt far and wide. She will agree that a Party function should be handled in one way, then decide on the spot to do it in another. She will change plans at short notice. Spontaneity or plain forgetfulness could be explanations, save that Margaret Thatcher is neither spontaneous nor forgetful when it comes to timetables and performances. It is just that she will sometimes be contrary, perhaps simply to make the point that she is still in charge of her own life.

She can wield political power ruthlessly, but cares nothing for the trappings. Sirens and flashing blue lights are anathema to her view of how a British Prime Minister should proceed through the traffic. On her first visit to Washington as Prime Minister, she was breathless and excited at the cacophony and size of the police presence, which would even include sending squad cars racing down the runway alongside her RAF VC10 until it was airborne. In Finchley, she has banned such overt police presence for herself and ordered that traffic flows should not be altered on her behalf. A policeman spotting her car and injudiciously countermanding the traffic signals to speed her on her way will bring the Prime Minister leaning sharply forward from the back of her Daimler and demanding: 'Why did that happen?' Chief Constables in other parts of the country who sometimes go for over-enthusiastic displays of police power do not create the favourable impression on her which they expect. What impress her are effectiveness and efficiency, not line upon line of police officers.

As I began to work with her it was as if an ever greater gulf was opening between the woman I knew and the one who was being seen by the nation. During my early months with her in Finchley in 1982, she was low in the opinion polls and much reviled by large sections of the media. This fuelled my desire to let people see what the real Margaret Thatcher was like. But she would refuse to allow this other, personal side of her to be shown. An example of this softer aspect can be seen in her attitude towards children; the child who knocks uninvited at the door of the constituency office at 212 Ballards Lane will find it easier to gain entry than will many Conservative MPs wishing to get into 10 Downing Street. One tiny girl who knocked wanting to see her left with a bouquet of flowers presented earlier to Margaret Thatcher, together with a photograph of the Prime Minister and herself taken by me. 'These flowers were given to me,' said the Prime Minister, sweeping them from the desk. 'But I know that the people who gave them would not mind me giving them to you.' She then instructed that a photograph be taken of her and the child, but a personal one which was not to go to the media. It was a similar story with a small lad from Newcastle who had come to Finchley to live with his uncle and who kept knocking, wanting to see the Prime Minister. He was repeatedly told to come back another day, until Margaret learned that her staff were keeping him away in order to protect her. The lad was invited in, and later went home delightedly with a photograph of himself and the Prime Minister.

There are other things that Margaret Thatcher feels to be taboo in public, such as any sign of tears. It's a fact that women cry more easily than men, but as she is our first woman Prime Minister no one, neither she herself nor the electorate, seems to be able to deal with anything more than a moistened cheek on very special occasions. But weep she can, as on one night at the Commons in 1980. It was just before the 10 p.m. vote and Ian Gow, the Conservative MP who was then her Parliamentary Private Secretary, asked a handful of fellow Conservative MPs to join the Prime Minister in her office when the vote was over. 'It's going to be difficult,' he said. 'It's the hand-over of power in Rhodesia tonight.' One MP recalls arriving to find Margaret Thatcher holding a glass of whisky, her favourite drink in the evening, and sitting in front of a huge television set watching the ITN news. The moment came when the Union flag was lowered for the last time in Rhodesia, and tears rolled down Margaret Thatcher's face. After apologising for her weeping, she explained: 'The poor Queen. To think of her having to hand over. Do you realise the number of colonies that have been handed over from the British Empire since she came to the throne?'

Another aspect of Margaret Thatcher's character is that she just does not gossip about other politicians, though many of those politicians, most of whom are male, make this part of their staple diet. She has no desire to hear every piece of tittle-tattle about her colleagues, as was the case, for example, with Harold Wilson. (She does, however, share a little of his passion for news of the writers and influential personalities in the media.) As a result of this lack of interest in gossip, she can often be very innocent about some of her fellow Conservative MPs. In the company of her political favourites (those who are 'one of us', as she puts it) she can wax forth with generous praise for the speaking or writing talents of a Minister who does not share the depth of her right-wing beliefs. After a slight pause, one of those with her might say: 'Yes – but of course he is not one of us.' She will look surprised at what was to all save her quite common knowledge. 'Really!' she will exclaim with genuine surprise. In the absence of an appetite for gossip, she relies primarily on the official channel of communication between her and her MPs: the Conservative Whips' Office.

She can be brusquely efficient with those who are paid to work for her, but full-hearted and generous with others outside the political world. A close aide once described her as 'slim with gratitude', and that sums up her relationship with the professionals around her. She expects them to be sharp, fast and efficient. Yet there is a side to her character and human responses that is very caring. To the cynic, any brain smart enough to get its owner to the top of politics' greasy pole and keep her there by winning three successive General Elections has got to be so canny that the human gestures and feelings of normal folk are simply worn like clothes. Certainly, Margaret Thatcher is blessed with an exceptional level of brain-power. Yet she is in her private life in Finchley a living example of the neighbourly and charitable ideal which she urges on the nation.

She has befriended a young, mentally handicapped girl from Manchester whom she met during a visit to the North of England in 1984 and to whom she writes regularly from 10 Downing Street. In Finchley, much of her charitable efforts are directed towards helping John Groom's, a home for the physically and mentally disabled. I have seen her drop to her knees at the side of the hydrotherapy pool in a Finchley school to talk with the severely disabled children and rise half-soaked and totally careless of it. Her deeply held belief is that we all have a moral duty to help those less fortunate than ourselves and that this is best done by us as individuals, not by shrugging it off on to the State. She shuns publicity for her charitable work, and at the very mention of a camera among the disabled she will become ferociously protective.

For me as her agent in Finchley, this refusal to countenance publicity connected with charity could be as infuriating and frustrating as her refusal to allow publication of other pictures, such as those of her and the children who arrive at the door of her Finchley headquarters. Clearly, I wanted everyone in the constituency to see their MP as the warm-hearted woman she can be and not as the heartless virago some sections of the media had made her. The events that followed her attendance at the charitable 'Saints and Sinners' lunch in London were typically galling for me as the Finchley agent. The Saints and Sinners raised £100,000 for charity and 10 per cent went to Margaret Thatcher to be forwarded to charities of her choice. A few days after the lunch she phoned me to recall her visit some weeks earlier to a Sea Scouts group in Finchley. She remembered that the roof leaked and organised a generous donation for its repair, but she preferred not to be identified. Even my hopes of pushing the news out when the Sea Scouts published their annual report were thwarted. The donation was wrapped up in a trust and her involvement has remained anonymous until today, as have similar donations to a church and to her old school in the town of Grantham.

It is not just money but her time that she gives, sometimes in the most unexpected ways and at the most unexpected moments. What other Prime Minister could start a fund-raising speech for the NSPCC with the words: 'When I was a Branch Secretary in this organisation . . .'? What other Prime Minister could, as she did after the Penlee lifeboat disaster, be so moved by a letter from the widow of the drowned cox as to travel to Cornwall under conditions of strictest secrecy to attend his funeral and meet with her?

Few people can match her for sustained workload, yet, hearing that an old lady in East Barnet whom she had known since 1959 had been unwell, she declared: 'Right, let's bring her down to the office.' As a cynical professional I thought this was a waste of my Member of Parliament's time and suggested that in view of the trouble and journey involved it was not a good idea. 'Quite right,' she said. 'I should have said that I'll go up there to see her.' As this would have required Special Branch officers going to the old lady's home in advance of the Prime Minister's visit to ensure that there were no security risks lurking in her home, I relented and we arranged to bring her to the Finchley offices. The Prime Minister spent twenty-five minutes in conversation with her about her sons and grandsons. It was twenty-five minutes that weren't going to win her any friends or votes in Finchley, and it happened to be at the end of a particularly gruelling week. But to Margaret Thatcher the woman was a friend and loyal supporter, so nothing was too much trouble. I later learned that the old lady had been at Margaret Thatcher's adoption meeting in 1959 when she was picked as the

Conservative candidate for the seat, and had been one of those who voted for her. For Margaret Thatcher, loyalty is a two-way street.

This old lady is just one of Finchley's many recipients of a gift at Christmas from Margaret and Denis Thatcher. Nor are these merely the House of Commons 'souvenir' presents that in the run-up to Christmas so many MPs buy in bulk. (These machine politicians and their staffs can be seen each year struggling under dozens of boxes of House of Commons mints, crates of House of Commons sherry and wine and cartons of House of Commons table mats.) The old lady's gift is individually selected, and the same thoughtfulness goes into the dozens of other personal presents from Margaret and Denis Thatcher.

Caring for others and generosity of spirit are not, according to Margaret Thatcher, virtues that can be created by the apparatus of the State or shuffled off on to it. As she said in a speech to St Lawrence of Jewry in London in 1981: 'There is a need for more generosity in our national life, but generosity is born in the hearts of men and women. It cannot be manufactured by politicians and assuredly it will not flourish if politicians foster the illusion that the exercise of compassion can be left to officials.'

It may well be that few people recognise this Margaret Thatcher. Even now, the sobriquet from the Russians of the 'Iron Lady' is still seen by many Britons as describing the essential woman. Of course, the political Margaret Thatcher is as tough as steel and can be as unyielding. But the private Margaret Thatcher is as sensitive and thoughtful as the next person, and perhaps more so.

By the time the 1983 General Election was approaching, it was clear to me that in Finchley the gap was at its narrowest between the real Margaret Thatcher and the one whom most of the rest of Britain seemed to see. For the election campaign I prepared a news sheet called 'The Finchley Leader', and the main article on the front page, written by local newspaper editor Dennis Signy, reflected much of the way I was beginning to see her:

A Russian leader nicknamed Margaret Thatcher the Iron Lady. Another world figure dubbed her 'The best man in the Cabinet'. A Westminster wag called her Tina – meaning There Is No Alternative.

But to the people of Finchley she is Margaret Thatcher, the caring, compassionate Member of Parliament for the past two decades.

The tough descriptions of the MP for Finchley are in fact a compliment but most local people find it hard to recognise this face of Margaret Thatcher. . . .

Although she has established a reputation as Britain's finest leader since Churchill and travels the globe she still tells residents of the Grange Estate in East Finchley that if world leaders want to meet her in early December they will have to take second place to the senior citizens' annual Christmas party. . . .

Go on a walkabout with Mrs Thatcher on her home patch and you will see a different face of the Iron Lady.

In recent weeks she has chatted about snooker with a young admirer she met in the street. She discussed the problems of bringing up young children with a mum in Ballards Lane.

When she met a centenarian in North Finchley last month they chatted about the opening of Tower Bridge, the era of horse-drawn carriages and the dramatic changes in the world since Mrs Thatcher's own childhood as the daughter of a thriving small shopkeeper in a market town.

One thing the two ladies had in common . . . a respect for thrift and hard work.

Of course, to the cynic, words from an election news sheet may seem tainted. The reaction to televised pictures of Margaret Thatcher with children is sometimes the accusation that the shots are 'posed'. But her spontaneous caring side can be well illustrated by two events. One involves her as MP for Finchley and the other as Prime Minister.

On polling day in the 1987 General Election, the home of Rosemary Renouf, one of Margaret Thatcher's Party workers in Finchley who was heavily pregnant, was used as a committee room. Margaret had arrived there early in the day, leaving at 11 a.m. only when Rosemary Renouf went into labour and the ambulance arrived. She was not in labour for long, and the news that she had given birth to a daughter, Margaret, was broken over the lunch table in the constituency headquarters. The other Margaret clapped her hands joyfully and, carried away in the excitement of the moment, declared that she must visit Rosemary Renouf in hospital there and then. As the Special Branch headed for the hospital to prepare the way, Margaret called a halt. She had wanted to go there as a woman and friend, but was clearly appalled by the chaos her arrival as Prime Minister would bring to the hospital. 'It's only hours after the birth,' she said. 'The last thing Rosemary will want to see is all of us.' Yet again, the instincts of the woman were overruled by the role of Prime Minister.

The second event occurred just after she slid into her Daimler outside 10 Downing Street to go to meet a visiting Head of State as he landed at London's Heathrow Airport. As the car pulled into the London traffic, she overheard the driver and a Special Branch guard exchanging news concerning one of the Number 10 cleaning ladies who had been mugged the night before and was in hospital. 'What's that?' demanded the Prime Minister. The news was recounted to her, whereupon she instructed the driver to go straight to the London hospital where the woman was recovering.

The same spontaneity broke out from under her self-discipline when she heard that Jim, the doorkeeper at 10 Downing Street, had decided to stay in his job for an extra twelve months. His reason: he wanted to be there to open the most famous door in the world for Margaret Thatcher when she chalked up her third successive General Election victory. Hearing the rumours of his reason for staying on, she went down from the private flat at the top of Number 10 to the black and white marble-floored hall that lies behind that black front door, and steered the conversation to his retirement. When he confirmed the story, she put her hands on the old man's shoulders, and with each 'Thank you' from her his cheeks grew redder with embarrassment and pleasure.

Margaret Thatcher's childhood teddy bear, scruffy, worn and among the most widely travelled teddies in the world, has been lent to many exhibitions in aid of charity, but what is not so well known is her affection for small, cuddly and live animals. Only once has she been publicly photographed with a dog – and that belonged to someone else – while she was holidaying in the West Country in 1986. However, the fluffy, overfed Number 10 Downing Street mouser owed to her a three-year extension of his working life. Officials decided that the old, fat cat was no longer capable of performing his mouse-catching duties. On grounds of cost-effectiveness he was to be despatched, a victim of market forces. Margaret intervened, and his exile was halted. Among friends in Finchley, she will play for twenty minutes with their golden retriever, rolling it on to its back, tickling it, and as oblivious as the animal to the rest of the world. There was an air of incredulity among the media when news got out that a stray cat had turned up on the doorstep at Chequers and had been taken in to be fed on scraps from the kitchen and to sleep on the sofa. Another example of the public image and the reality being two entirely different things.

She is more superstitious than the science graduate from Oxford would have the world believe. She has what are for her 'lucky' dresses. When she met a group of Asian businessmen who told her that they will take no major decision in their lives without consulting their Eastern seer for his views, her interest was more than polite. There are no days in her diary when she will not take a decision because a self-styled clairvoyant has warned against it, but it is clearly a subject that interests her.

Though she holds the office of Prime Minister, she remains an aware hostess even when in the company of her Ministers and MPs. All the Prime Ministers who preceded her were as likely as she to issue spur-of-the-moment invitations to fellow politicians to return to the flat for a late-night drink. None, however, can have acted as she does when her guests are seated in 10 Downing Street – raiding the freezer for a three-course meal.

The combination of surprise and embarrassment that this produced in her guests in the early days of her Premiership was probably equalled only during the Falklands War at the conclusion of a meeting of the War Cabinet. She left her chair at the Cabinet table and raced out, leaving the other members collecting together their papers. They walked out to find the Prime Minister descending the stairs with a sliced fruit cake. It had been a long meeting and, even though she is Prime Minister, the role of hostess is always at the back of her mind.

At times she can also be a woman who knows not only of the loneliness of supreme political power, but of personal loneliness, too, upstairs in the flat over Number 10 without her family. The mask slipped to give a glimpse of this loneliness one night at the House of Commons, when the organisers of her Conservative Association's dining club presented her with a gift, a clock. Usually, and like most politicians who are given a present, Margaret Thatcher will unwrap the gift there and then. It is not just politeness; there are often many people present who have contributed towards the gift but who have not seen what has been bought. On this occasion, she made it clear that she was in no hurry to leave her hosts, and added that she would take the present back to the flat to open later that night. What the men and women at the dining club did not know, and what she did not reveal, was that although there were plenty of Despatch Boxes waiting for her back there, there was no family. That weekend, son Mark was in America, daughter Carol was away working and husband Denis was in Portugal playing golf. So the Prime Minister, MP for Finchley and world leader, was driven back to the flat late at night to unwrap the present alone.

There is that punctilious correctness about her of a person with great respect for tradition. She may often feel impatience with Bernard Weatherill, the Speaker of the Commons, but she will unfailingly bow low to him as she enters and leaves the chamber, because he is the representative of authority there. Ironically, other MPs who have a much higher personal regard for Bernard Weatherill will not give so much as a nod in his direction. This exactitude with all rules, formalities and conventions can result in moments of humility for her from which she seems to derive personal pleasure, as at the start of the 1987 election campaign. She walked into her adoption meeting at Finchley with no rosette on her dress. Her audience was adoring. Before the most devout of all

Finchley's Conservatives stood the woman who was bidding to be Prime Minister for the third time in succession, as well as their Member of Parliament. It was inconceivable that they would fail to adopt Margaret Hilda Thatcher as their candidate. But not until the adoption procedure was completed and Margaret Thatcher was their official candidate did she lift her handbag to the table, take out her blue rosette with 'Margaret Thatcher for Finchley' emblazoned on it in gold letters, and pin it to her dress.

As the years passed in working as agent for Margaret Thatcher, it became inevitable that I should draw comparisons between her and the other two Conservative Leaders I had met, Sir Alec Douglas Home (now Lord Home of the Hirsel) and Edward Heath. Sir Alec called me in 1964 to his home on the Douglas estate in Scotland. I was greeted at the door by his son David, setting off with a gun over his shoulder, and by the Prime Minister's wife, Elizabeth, with a grandchild over her shoulder. Sir Alec welcomed me in his study, where he was seated with a podgy and unknown young man who in later years was to become famous: Nigel Lawson, the second Chancellor of the Exchequer in Margaret Thatcher's Government.

I was then the Conservative Trade Union Organiser in Scotland and the reason for my summons to Sir Alec was to brief him on how the working-class vote was expected to break down in Scotland in the coming General Election. In the early 1960s there was still something called the 'deferential vote' in Scotland, coming from that portion of the working class who thought they *should* vote for the Conservatives, especially if the Conservative candidate appealing for their votes owned a lot of land and had forefathers who had been politicians. The rationale of the 'deferential vote' was that God had made these Conservatives in a superior mould and thus they were entitled to govern. Sir Alec was an aristocrat who was also a gentleman, but the days of the 'deferential vote' were passing rapidly and the Conservative Party was on its way to a more meritocratic regime, beginning with the choice of Edward Heath from the lower middle classes as its Leader. The great irony, of course, was that Sir Alec had more of the common touch during his Premiership than did Edward Heath. Margaret Thatcher has it in quantities which neither could dream of, let alone exude.

My own experience with Edward Heath during his first tour of Scotland as Party Leader served to underline just how difficult he found it at times to get on with fellow politicians, let alone the ordinary folk he expected to vote for him. When he came to Scotland I was the agent in West Renfrewshire and he was to visit the constituency being fought for the Conservatives by Alex Fletcher, who was to go on to become an MP and junior Minister in Margaret Thatcher's Government. It was a full day's visit and John MacGregor, one of Edward Heath's personal staff who also became a member of Margaret Thatcher's Government, briefed me over a cup of coffee in advance of the great man's arrival. He warned me that Heath was slow to get going in the morning and must not on any account be upset. This proved to be an inadequate warning for what was to follow. Edward Heath said virtually nothing, save for those grunts for which he became well known but which hardly passed for conversation. Even when we arrived at our first engagement near Linwood, he appeared not to know even Alex Fletcher's name, let alone mine.

With an hour to go before he and about a hundred others were due to start lunch, he did say one thing to me: that no one was to sit down for lunch, but rather they were to circulate with a stand-up buffet. The startled catering manager said it was impossible in the time available to turn the sit-down meal into a buffet, but that he would speed up the entire four courses so that the lunch would be over in forty-five minutes. This would leave everyone to mix and mingle in the remaining time available. It was a formidable task, but was achieved without mishap and to the minute. Despite my attempt to explain this remarkable feat to Edward Heath, he walked straight past the catering manager on the way out without so much as expressing thanks.

The rest of the day was spent with Edward Heath despatching angrily worded telegrams to the then Prime Minister Harold Wilson with demands to know why nationalised industry prices were going up in view of the fact that there was now a prices and incomes policy. The result was that at 8 p.m., when Heath was due to make his main speech of the day in Paisley, he was still waiting for a reply from Harold Wilson, and by 8.11 p.m. the band in the hall was playing 'Scotland the Brave' for the umpteenth time as his audience wondered what had happened. When he finally did arrive, his speech was excellent and the evening ended with him uncorking a bottle of Glenfiddich whisky in his hotel room and enquiring if he had 'done any good' that day and whether he could do any more to help. Along with the uncorking of the bottle, a more agreeable face of Edward Heath was also uncorked. But it had been a difficult and disappointing day.

Such behaviour would be inconceivable in Margaret Thatcher. She could never forget to thank the entire kitchen staff, let alone the catering manager, keep an audience waiting or forget a name. She has a natural and real interest in people. She will lean forward eagerly to listen, and has a memory that will recall eighteen months later the name of a constituent's son or daughter and where they work.

She has, too, a gentle woman's touch. She was once introduced to a soldier at Sweets Way, Whetstone, part of the Mill Hill Barracks in north London where 600 soldiers and their wives live. On this occasion she had been invited there to become an honorary member of the mess. The young soldier, who had gone through the Falklands campaign, froze with embarrassment when faced with the Prime Minister. She simply touched his arm, led him a step or two with her and quietly spoke of how she, too, had been to Tumbledown on the Falklands, although he must have seen it at 5 a.m. when the advance began. Within seconds he had thawed, and was talking not with the Prime Minister but with the woman within.

This type of personal contact brought Joy Robilliard, formerly secretary to the assassinated Conservative MP Airey Neave, to work with her at 10 Downing Street after his death. The murder of Neave, killed by an IRA bomb as he drove out of the Commons underground car park in March 1979, was an event of as tragic and unsettling proportions for Margaret Thatcher as for Joy Robilliard.

[43]

He had been a close personal and political friend, her campaign manager during her bid for the Party Leadership in 1975, and a man of great personal courage. He was the first Allied officer to escape from Colditz, the fortress in which prisoners of war were kept by the Germans and from which they had claimed no one could free themselves.

Hours after the IRA bomb exploded under Airey Neave's car, Joy Robilliard went to her home in north London and vowed she would never again return to the Commons and the political world. Two months later, after the 1979 General Election, she received a phone call from Number 10 asking her to go to see the new Prime Minister. Margaret Thatcher talked to her about Airey Neave's death, explained that his widow was being made a life peeress at her request, and all the time walked Joy Robilliard round the building, pausing in first one room and then another to ask her opinion about curtains and wallpapers before finally opening a door and saying: 'This is your office, Joy, where I hope you will be my constituency secretary.' By then Joy Robilliard was captivated. She has been there ever since.

'She is beautiful, gay, very kind and thoughtful –
and a jolly good cook.'　　(Denis Thatcher)

4

THE WOMAN

_____

A RECENTLY ARRIVED phenomenon in the world of Westminster is that of political groupies – women who are attracted to male politicians, or rather who are attracted not so much to the man as to the political power which he exudes. If there is a similar phenomenon of men who are attracted to women political leaders in this country, then I have not yet observed it in the presence of Margaret Thatcher. It may be that such male groupies exist, but they would not get within sight of her before she was brushing them aside with a well-aimed handbag, or chilling them with a look from flashing blue eyes.

This is not to say that she is oblivious to the attractions of men or of her attractiveness to men. Given the choice between two men who were equal in all respects save for their looks, one can assume that she would prefer the company of the more handsome individual. She knows that she is attractive and enjoys the effect of her own striking good looks. When David Owen was still in the Labour Party, he described her just before the 1979 General Election as a heady mixture of whisky and perfume. In the mood of pre-election hysteria, the remark was in some quarters interpreted as a wicked attempt by Dr Owen to smear her. Whatever his motives, she confided shortly afterwards that she was not at all offended by the

[47]

description but quite flattered by it. Her reaction may have had a little to do with the fact that the comment came from the good-looking Dr Owen. Perhaps it was President Mitterrand of France who came closest to defining that mixture of sexuality and political power which she emanates when he said: 'She has the eyes of Caligula and the mouth of Marilyn Monroe.'

Her penchant for good-looking men, and particularly for those in uniform, was to become the subject of much comment among her Ministers during her early years in 10 Downing Street, but this was hardly a taste that she had developed in later years. Her husband Denis was an army major, and even in his seventies retains a striking military bearing.

She does not use her femininity to get her way in the Government, or indeed in Finchley. She has no need to. But her liking for good-looking men seems to be increased if they are capable of the lightest of flirtations with her – so light that it would never be construed as overt, but possibly as something to do with the 'chemistry' between two people. The notion that she reacts chemically or instinctively for or against people is not far-fetched. Others who have worked with her have observed, as I did, that she will often seem to make an instant and instinctive judgement on someone. Having reacted instinctively, it is unlikely that she will change her mind.

Of course, the implicit power of her political office is sufficient to secure her way without the need for any so-called 'feminine wiles'. She does not even drop her gaze as so many women do out of a shyness, genuine or affected, that they find useful to demonstrate at times. Instead, the pale blue eyes – paler and more Arctic with the passing years – stare into the other's face. Rather than look down the eyes are much more likely to narrow, such as when a journalist friend of mine interviewed her and brought the discussion round to her retirement. He recalls: 'The eyes narrowed, the coldness of the eyes became quite terrifying and the very temperature in the room seemed to chill.'

Since she moved into 10 Downing Street, the nation has seen the face of its first woman Prime Minister, rarely the face of the woman and never the child that lives on in her. The girl that is still there stepped out briefly when she used the word 'naughty' in talking about the bombing of the Grand Hotel in Brighton in October 1984. She was 'naughty', she said, to forget to hang up her suit in the Grand Hotel in the early hours shortly before the IRA bomb exploded there. Trawl through all her speeches, interviews and other publicly spoken words since she went into politics, and 'naughty' is one word that will not be found. It has undertones of the childhood world of Margaret Hilda Roberts, and her father frowning at his daughter in the grocer's shop in Grantham one morning over her failure to hang up her school uniform the night before.

The shadow of the schoolgirl can be seen, too, sometimes in the early hours when, with people she knows, she will kick off her shoes and sit at the foot of the best-looking man in the room.

This almost childlike side to Margaret Thatcher is a total contrast to the public face known to the world from its television screens. She has been portrayed at times, and certainly during her early years in 10 Downing Street, as something of a 'fishwife', behaving, whether at home or abroad, as if she were shouting over a garden fence. In fact, in the early days of her Premiership the label 'fishwife' was used on private occasions by at least one Cabinet Minister to describe her. It seemed to sum up the way much of the world saw her: a non-stop talker, bossy and unwilling to let a man get a word in edgeways even if he was a world leader.

Her alleged verbosity never seemed to me to be any stronger a character trait than it is in most other politicians, but it was an allegation that clearly hurt her enough for her to give some thought as to its possible accuracy. She told me that she had taken the criticism very much to heart and had considered it seriously. Subsequently, she promised herself that she would not be the first to speak at European Council meetings. Then, without a trace of amusement, she later explained what had happened when she adopted this approach at the next gathering of the heads of Common Market governments: 'But when I said nothing all the men just sat there and said nothing, so I had to say something.'

[49]

These contradictions between the Margaret Thatcher known to me and the one known to much of the world stem in large part from the role she was compelled by circumstances to act out as first woman Leader of the Opposition and then as first woman Prime Minister. Perhaps inevitably, from the day she became Conservative Leader in 1975 it was necessary for her advisers to project what, in the clichés of mass communication, are seen as the 'manly' qualities of decisiveness, firmness and resolve rather than the 'feminine' ones. It was a reasonable enough decision, because in those days the reactions of the British electorate to a woman leader, let alone to a woman Prime Minister, were untested. Nor was the economic and industrial legacy which she found on reaching 10 Downing Street exactly conducive to the feminine touch.

Though she does not use her femininity to get her way, its existence presents difficulties for some men, often those from public schools who do not feel easy in the company of the opposite sex, and in the absence of this *savoir faire* the aspiring young Conservative MP can be at a disadvantage, as at least one of their number at Westminster has recognised to his cost.

This MP was called on by Party managers to help the Prime Minister as an aide at 10 Downing Street in what was expected to be the run-up to his appointment as her Parliamentary Private Secretary. However, it was decided that he was not the right man for the job when he kept forgetting things for her – not important items like documents or speeches, but the thoughtful precautions such as a woollen wrap in case it got chilly on out-of-town engagements. As Margaret Thatcher herself once said: 'I like to be made a fuss of by a lot of chaps.'

Sometimes I would fail to recognise the need to take into account her femininity and sensitivity to the way others see her. For example, one evening at Chequers she and I were putting together the constituency news sheet, 'The Finchley Leader', in readiness for the 1983 General Election. Her daughter Carol was there and the three of us laid out on the floor the possible pictures for the news sheet. I kept pushing forward a picture of Margaret Thatcher with two well-known figures from the constituency. Without comment and almost surreptitiously, she kept pulling the picture out and putting it to one side. When Margaret left the room I turned to Carol and asked her if she knew why her mother did not want me to use the photograph. Carol said: 'Look closely at the picture. It shows her with a double chin.'

Margaret Thatcher herself once said: 'I may be Prime Minister, but the one thing I will insist on is being feminine.' She likes to be given flowers, although she has no particular preference. Simply receiving them serves to reaffirm her femininity in what remains essentially a male world.

It has been said that she was born with a man's head on a woman's body, but she does have a need for some 'women's talk', such as discussions about fashion, make-up and children. These matters are talked over with daughter Carol; with Joy, her long-serving constituency secretary; with 'Crawfie', former secretary to Sir David Wolfson, who was head of her private office; with Christine Wall, her political press secretary and confidante (now at the Central Office Press Department); and with Sue Thurlow, wife of the Finchley Conservative Association Chairman.

But there is a need for 'women's talk' at a level that goes deeper than mere discussion of bows and belts and which cannot be satisfied by men, certainly not those in her Cabinet. It was this need that led Margaret Thatcher, in the aftermath of the Brighton bombing, to meet frequently with Lynda Chalker, then her Junior Transport Minister. They discussed every detail of what was being done to help Margaret Tebbit, the wife of the Party Chairman, whose spine had been shattered in the bombing. Money was buying all that it could for Margaret Tebbit; hands had been put into pockets by the Party to raise cash for house adaptations and a lift. But there was a deep personal distress in Margaret Thatcher that required discussion with other women.

Her compassion is no less genuine for not being worn on her sleeve. Time and again I have known of letters drafted for her to send to the bereaved which she has torn up in exasperation, usually without the aide who drafted it ever knowing, to rewrite it herself. Letters to women, especially mothers, in her constituency will often go out with a handwritten postscript from her.

Margaret Thatcher also demonstrated a deep concern for Norman Tebbit after the bombing, which intruded right into the Cabinet Room. He was hobbling and half doubled with his injuries, with a hole in his side that refused to heal. She was aware every time she saw him that the crippled figure could have been her had the bomb been planted a few yards differently, and that she above all others in the Cabinet had been the IRA's target. She was so anxious to please and help him that it began to infuriate some Cabinet Ministers. One recalls: 'It was during a Cabinet Committee and Norman was being quite irrational on the matter under discussion. She kept trying to agree with him but no one else round the table would. Then, to our amazement, he stood up and half stomped, half limped out of the Cabinet Room. This was before the Westland Affair and the walk-out by Michael Heseltine. To our greater astonishment, she stood up and rushed out of the room, pausing only to explain "We must understand Norman's problems."'

Margaret Thatcher's patience with Norman Tebbit was not boundless, of course. She made him Party Chairman and some of her Cabinet colleagues say she did so partly out of that sense of guilt that had her running out of the Cabinet Room after him. Whatever the reason, no sooner had she given him the job than she was behaving as if she no longer wanted him there. The reasons for her mental turnabout on Norman Tebbit are as unclear as those which, when Leon Brittan resigned from the Cabinet, made her look forward to his return, then refuse to acknowledge his existence for almost three years or have him back in the Cabinet. Eventually, and totally unexpectedly, she made him a European Commissioner.

Perhaps the best explanation of this apparently contrary side of Margaret came from Lord Hailsham, former Lord Chancellor. 'You've got to put her in the same category as Bloody Mary, Queen Elizabeth I, Queen Anne and Queen Victoria,' he said. 'Well, she does remind me more of Queen Elizabeth I, out of those four. Her handling of men is not dissimilar. I mean, if you had been a courtier of Queen Elizabeth I, you would never know quite whether you were going to get the treatment of an admired friend, or a poke in the eye with an umbrella.'

Margaret Thatcher's relationship with the Queen has been the subject of much speculation, none of it arising from anything Margaret has said. Even in private she will say only of the Queen: 'I am her most loyal subject.' Whatever the truth of the speculation of strains between monarch and Prime Minister over policies early in the Thatcher Government, my instincts tell me that there was none during the Falklands War. With Prince Andrew flying helicopter sorties off the Falklands, the Queen was as much a mother as a monarch, and there was an affinity and understanding between them on Tuesdays when the Prime Minister went to Buckingham Palace for her regular audience.

Since she became Prime Minister there has been a network of women behind Margaret Thatcher whose names never get into the newspapers but upon whom she depends. Crawfie and Joy Robilliard are more than just secretaries. They help her with all the personal day-to-day problems that are bound to afflict the first woman Prime Minister. It is Crawfie and Joy who will return from London's Oxford Street with make-up and, perhaps, a Marks & Spencer shepherd's pie for the Number 10 freezer. It is Crawfie and Joy who are charged by the Prime Minister with the purchase of the personal gifts she would like to buy if she were free to go shopping herself, as she was in her pre-Premier days and never will be again. Today a security net prevents her from just popping to the shops, as she was able to do even as recently as 1974 when she was Education Secretary, when she would stop off in London's King's Road some evenings on the way home from work.

The public often assumes that the Civil Service arranges for all these personal details to be looked after for a Prime Minister. In fact, the Civil Service is capable of doing almost anything for the Prime Minister, but it draws a sharp line at assisting the holder of the office in any activities it considers to be non-Prime Ministerial. It is the ubiquitous Joy Robilliard, for instance, who arranges payment for the cleaner of the flat over 10 Downing Street; most people would think, as I did at first, that the State pays for that. In fact the Civil Service will happily arrange for staff to tidy up behind Margaret Thatcher when she is Prime Minister downstairs, but as soon as she goes up to the flat any mess she makes is her own responsibility. Margaret Thatcher would not have it any other way.

Similarly, Joy looks after the diary of Denis Thatcher, making note of his appointments in order that he can plan to spend time with his wife, although he insists that nothing more is done for him either by her or by anyone else. He looks after all his own mail.

Margaret Thatcher seems to have no real female friends in the Commons among the MPs there. Lynda Chalker, Virginia Bottomley and Edwina Currie all have with her that common bond that comes from being one of a minority in a man's world, but none is a close friend. Margaret's sister Muriel, who married a farmer and has shunned reflected publicity, speaks regularly to her on the telephone; but there is not a frequent personal contact between them, though Muriel does attend some private parties at Chequers.

It has often been to older women that Margaret Thatcher has looked for friendship, certainly in her early years in 10 Downing Street: to Lady Tilney, for instance, wife of ex-Conservative MP Sir John Tilney. For years, she would make an appearance in 10 Downing Street almost every day. Another example is Lady Glover, wife of another ex-Conservative MP whose home in Switzerland the Thatchers used to use for holidays during the early years in power.

There are some things that even Crawfie and Joy cannot do for Margaret Thatcher – such as buying clothes. So the proprietors of London's fashion shops are invited to go to see her early some evenings. A condition of the invitation is that no use is made of it to create publicity. Both clothes and jewellery in themselves mean less to her than is thought. She will always insist on being faultlessly turned out, but often behind her immaculate appearance is a frantic rush, with her and Carol swapping clothes and jewellery when either is in a flap. As a child she was used to her seamstress mother altering her sister's cast-offs to fit her, and her approach to clothes remains businesslike. She will occasionally bestow compliments on other women for the way they are turned out, but an expression such as 'Don't you look glamorous my dear' is rare. Nor will she ever respond to compliments made to her with anything more than a simple 'Thank you'.

Her favourite pieces of jewellery are pearls, and most of those she owns have been given to her by Denis. He bought her the double string of cultured pearls when the twins were born. There is one other favourite – a large bracelet of coloured stones which clanks on the desk as she signs papers.

A hairdresser calls regularly at 10 Downing Street, usually before 9 a.m. But there are special weeks when he has to call more often, such as those involving visits from other Heads of State. It has also been known for an afternoon's itinerary to be changed for the sake of attention by a hairdresser. This happened just before the 1983 General Election. Elaborate arrangements had been made for her to fly by helicopter from her final election campaign engagement in the Isle of Wight to Mill Hill Barracks in north London on the edge of her constituency. I had been asked to arrange for the correct grid reference to be passed to 10 Downing Street, and Brigadier Rolf James at the barracks was on alert for his special visitor. Twenty-four hours before she was due to arrive, the entire programme was changed and it was announced to her staff that the Prime Minister would fly by helicopter to Battersea in London before driving to Finchley. The reason emerged shortly afterwards: Margaret Thatcher had remembered that she needed to see her hairdresser on the eve of poll so that she looked her best when the election results were announced.

She is as scrupulous about not attending to her make-up or hair in public as she is about keeping her nails always medium in length and shining with clear varnish. Naturally, at the Finchley Conservative Association office after our meetings on a Friday I would leave the room whenever she opened her handbag and reached for her comb and lipstick. But other men found, as I did, that the operation of fixing hair and make-up was completed so quickly that sometimes it was over before you could reach the door. I suspect that, like me, other men have eventually given up trying to race to the door, simply averting their gaze for a moment as the brief procedure is disposed of.

This speed in attending to her appearance is illustrated by an exchange between Margaret Thatcher and Norman St John Stevas during the early years of the Government when he was still in her Cabinet. Towards the end of a meeting of Ministers chaired by the Prime Minister, Norman St John Stevas was showing clear signs of agitation, fidgeting and seeming to want to get away. Eventually, she looked at him and said that he appeared anxious to escape. He replied that she was quite correct; he did want to leave because he had a very important engagement at Covent Garden Opera House. She replied that she was going to the opera as well. Norman St John Stevas, always sartorially splendid with an Edwardian elegance, told her: 'Yes Prime Minister – but it takes me a great deal longer to get ready than you.'

Male politicians are generally oblivious to their surroundings except in as much as they reflect their status. Margaret Thatcher, on the other hand, has always had an awareness of surroundings, which leads her to comment privately about them. In the case of one hotel to which visits are made regularly in Finchley as part of the Conservative Association's annual routine, she finally told the management that it 'needs decorating properly'. She comments on and remembers wallpaper, carpets and light fittings in a way that no male politician of my acquaintance ever has. Only a woman Prime Minister, perhaps, would have walked out of a church hall in the constituency saying how impressed she was with the peach-coloured interior because it had a warmth about it that is just not felt with grey. Again, perhaps only a woman – and only one as thrifty as Margaret – would have said as she walked into the Finchley constituency office: 'Isn't this a remarkable carpet? It's been down here twelve years.'

Though she does not have a taste for political gossip, she does have an ear and a memory for the scraps of personal news about civil servants and their families which filter to her through Crawfie, Joy Robilliard and others. After one Cabinet meeting, she, Sir Robert (now Lord) Armstrong, the Cabinet Secretary, and Bernard Ingham, her Press Secretary, were allocating the tasks for different individuals to implement the decisions of the Cabinet. Somewhere towards the end of this process, the name of a civil servant was mentioned by Sir Robert and Bernard Ingham for a particular task. 'Do you really think so?' asked the Prime Minister. 'His wife has just had a miscarriage, you know, and I don't think this is the best time to ask him.' Neither man knew of their colleague's personal problem, and when they left the Prime Minister late that morning they puzzled as to how she knew.

She has her own warmth which simply does not, and cannot, come across in television appearances or newspaper interviews. On a visit to a factory she will listen to the views of a worker with the same interest as she will listen to those of a Cabinet Minister, and she also finds the time to be thoughtful to her staff. Once, while I was with her in the walled rose garden at Chequers – her favourite place in the building and its grounds – I spotted an iron table with a red telephone on it. What, I asked, was a telephone doing in the garden? 'I found it stopped the staff having to walk around to find me,' she said.

She is always a hostess, though sometimes too enthusiastic for Downing Street security staff. Most of all they recall the evening when they rushed, horrified, through the guests towards the Prime Minister who, then aged nearly sixty, was standing on a chair and heaving at a sash window that had become stuck. I have also seen her preparing for a Number 10 reception, bustling around with a bottle of scotch in one hand and a bottle of gin in the other, being trailed patiently by a civil servant seeking her signature for Government papers. With the civil servant still in tow, she suddenly declared from the small kitchen area that more heavy, chunky glasses were needed for the scotch. When Peter Taylor, the office manager at Number 10, said there were no more available, she reminded him about a small cupboard in the corridor that leads from Number 10 into Number 11 where the Chancellor of the

Exchequer, then Sir Geoffrey Howe, lived. 'But they are the Chancellor's glasses,' explained Peter Taylor. 'Never mind,' she said. 'He won't mind – get them out.'

At the official country residence she seems to become even more the hostess, perhaps because Chequers, given to Prime Ministers for all time by Lord Lee of Fareham in 1918, is more spacious a location for social occasions. In the winter, she personally ensures the comfort of her guests by picking log after log from the basket to throw them into the open fire. The three armed services take it in turns to supply personnel to look after the catering at Chequers and its occupants. But Margaret Thatcher insists on supervising the food and drinks, even though this is quite unnecessary. She fusses that the right knives are laid and that the napkins are in just the right place. She simply likes being involved and feeling that she has had a hand in the preparation of events for her guests.

Of course, the armed services have sometimes been known to slip up in the catering, but the one occasion they did so in Margaret Thatcher's presence says more about her than about them. Sir Geoffrey Howe, then Chancellor of the Exchequer, was at Chequers for dinner and an overawed naval Wren spilled soup down his suit. 'Oh my dear,' exclaimed the Prime Minister, 'are you all right?' The Chancellor of the Exchequer looked up from his wet lap to see that the anxious Margaret Thatcher was not addressing him but the Wren, who was on the point of tears.

'We must always beware of supposing that somehow we can get rid of our own moral duties by handing them over to the community.'   (Margaret Thatcher)

5

THATCHERISM

Just what is Thatcherism? However it is analysed and defined by political academics, it is recognised by the ordinary British voter as something distinctly different from the Conservatism that they have known during the rest of the twentieth century. With my working-class Glasgow background, the difference was both exciting and enticing to me. Thatcherism was the realisation of an instinctive feeling that had grown within me and many others. We now realise we spent most of our lives waiting for and willing Thatcherism to happen, for someone to give expression, life and shape to a set of beliefs and to have the moral courage to put them to work.

It was less than a year after her 1979 General Election victory that Margaret Thatcher began to define Thatcherism. At that time, though, her brand of politics had not been formally turned into an 'ism'. She told the first Airey Neave memorial lecture in London that the political philosophy of her close colleague and personal friend, assassinated a year earlier by the IRA, had been almost identical to hers: 'This philosophy does not, and cannot, exactly reflect that of any one great Conservative thinker or statesman of the past, for the obvious reason that our circumstances are utterly different from anything hitherto known.'

That was an early hint of what was to come. Then, in May 1980 she told the Conservative Women's Conference in London exactly what was her 'right kind of government'. She said:

When government does its job properly, people are free to do theirs.

The right kind of government ensures that people keep more of what they earn. That's why we've cut income tax at all levels. You spend your own money more wisely than governments. And people are more likely to take an interest in what they do and in the future of their company if they can share in its rewards.

Under the right kind of government, people are free and willing to accept personal responsibility. That's what helps people grow and mature; it strengthens the family; it leads to a tolerant and generous society. A generous society encourages talent and reaps the rewards for doing so. Academic excellence, for example, isn't just about elites. It's about raising teaching standards in a way that benefits every child. Business success isn't just a selfish aim. Profits spread beyond those who make them and bring jobs and prosperity.

The key to Thatcherism which has captured the support of all classes of British people is simple. It stresses the fact that it doesn't matter how humble your origins or background, effort, responsibility and aspiration will be the mark by which you will be judged and rewarded. This has irresistible appeal for a class-ridden country struggling to establish a new social order.

Margaret Thatcher's creed puts the 'evil' of inflation into its moral as well as its historical perspective. For over thirty years the value of the British currency has been eroding and the moral responsibility of the people with it.

Inflation is an insidious evil because its effects are slow to be seen and relatively painless in the short run. Yet it has a morally debilitating influence on all aspects of our national life. It reduces the value of savings, it undermines financial agreements, it stimulates hostility between workers and employers over matters of pay, it encourages debt and it diminishes the prospects of jobs. That is why I put its demise at the top of my list of economic priorities. It is, in my view, a moral issue, not just an economic one.

[62]

The eradication of inflation, then raging as a legacy of the 1974–9 Labour Government, has always been a moral imperative for her. I find it ironic that inflation rampaged under socialism, when it hits hardest at the weaker members of society least able to withstand its effects: the old, the sick and the dependent. Speaking during the last era of rampant inflation under Labour power, Margaret Thatcher spelled out why it had to be curbed.

> Inflation, like heavy taxation, reduces freedom. It denies people the dignity of planning their own lives. How can you provide for the future when you don't know what your savings or your occupational pension will be worth next year, let alone in five years? Planning, whether for a young family, a home of your own or for retirement, becomes difficult. And when people cannot plan for themselves, they are forced to look to the State.
>
> What will the level of State benefits be next year or the year after? Prospects depend not on personal effort but on the doubtful patronage of the State. The demand for more spending – but really for more inflation – gets built into the system.
>
> Income becomes something to vote for or to strike for, but not to work for. That's the vicious circle we must break.

Mrs Thatcher reacted typically in 1987 when, with the consumer boom raging, inflation began to move upwards again. The Chancellor of the Exchequer, Nigel Lawson, was unwilling to make the conquest of inflation his first priority. For at least six months she and the Chancellor tussled until he gave way and agreed that the pound should rise and interest rates, too, as high as was necessary to conquer inflation again.

It was the inheritance of runaway inflation from Labour that was in part responsible for what Margaret Thatcher called the 'patronage State' of the 1970s – a society where what you earned and therefore your standard of living were the results not of prudence or effort but of what pressure groups pressed for or the State bestowed. The 'patronage State' is the antithesis of the individual personal responsibility which she espouses.

The patronage State deprives people of dignity. Spending and inflation destroy what people achieve for themselves. It denies rewards and responsibility to the majority who want to work hard and look after their families. There's no morality in taxing away a man's ability to save and then offering him instead a State handout. If you take away the right to responsibility you actually undermine the family instead of supporting it.

But the real tragedy of the patronage State is that it lacks the means to be compassionate. It cannot look after those most in need. It cannot create the wealth to give a decent standard of living to those who really cannot look after themselves.

The drift to the patronage State, which suited socialists so well with their belief that everything in life, from housing to pensions, was best handled by them, had stemmed from what Margaret Thatcher called 'misplaced compassion'. She went on:

It was easier to demand State aid for a need than to face the problem that gave rise to it.

It was easier to prop up yesterday's industries rather than encourage the creation of tomorrow's.

It was easier to spend a little more, to tax a little more, to print a little more money, always a little more, than to create the wealth that was lacking.

It was easier to demonstrate – and call for the spending of other people's money – than to accept responsibility ourselves.

But is Thatcherism, as its critics claim, just the knee-jerk reaction of a housewife and grocer's daughter, a narrow, blinkered, selfish and grasping attitude to life? Or is it something more profound?

Margaret Thatcher has been described as the first fully committed Christian Prime Minister since Lord Salisbury, who died in 1903, and she is a more frequent attender at the small church at Chequers than her predecessors. I would argue that her political principles spring in large measure from her religious beliefs. However, her belief in a God has a practical expression, unlike the fervour of some of the 'born-again' Christians who inhabit Conservative Central Office and other posts close to the Prime Minister.

She does not, for example, follow the credo of Harvey Thomas, the Central Office guru on television presentation who is forever speaking of God. (Harvey happily recounts how, after he crashed through two floors of the Grand Hotel at Brighton after the 1984 IRA bombing and lay above a gaping hole five floors above ground level, he had a jolly conversation with God as the rubble poured down on him. He relates how he told God that although they had known each other for years, they would be unable to get together in Heaven just yet because his wife's baby was overdue and he was praying to see them both.) It is unusual to hear Margaret Thatcher speaking of God, but her origins in strict Methodism show through.

She likes to have around her politicians and aides who are deeply religious. Among these, apart from Harvey Thomas, are Professor Hugh Griffiths, head of her policy unit at 10 Downing Street; Keith Britto, head of Special Services at Conservative Central Office; Christine Wall, her Political Press Secretary; and John Gummer, a member of the Church of England Synod. Similarly, Michael Alison, the MP who was her Parliamentary Private Secretary from 1983 to 1987, was so strongly involved in the Church of England that he organised prayer meetings among MPs at Westminster, and I am an Elder of the Church of Scotland. Her own religious activities go beyond those that might be considered simply politic for a Prime Minister. For example, when I left Finchley she had attended no less than thirteen of the twenty-four Women's Day of Prayer meetings arranged there. She also made a special trip from Chequers one Sunday to attend the dedication service of St Paul's Church, Finchley at the height of the furore over the bombing of Libya.

I believe she has adopted the Church of England in part because it is less emotional than Methodism, and also because she is Prime Minister of Great Britain and Northern Ireland and it is the established Church. Despite that, she believes that sections of the Church of England have let the country down and detests so-called 'liberalism' in the Church as much as she dislikes socialism in politics. Faced with socialism in the Church of England, she is at her most ferocious, as when she meets with a local socialist CND-promoting vicar in Finchley. When he wanted to visit her at the Finchley Conservative Association office with two other members of CND, my advice was to make excuses and refuse to see them. But she insisted that she must see them, and when they arrived she opened by linking the minister's politics and advocacy of unilateral nuclear disarmament with the fact that his church was half empty on Sundays. Another churchman, who arrived to complain about government plans to liberalise Sunday trading, was asked if he supported the existing system under which his constituents could buy on a Sunday a magazine full of nude women disporting themselves, but could not buy a copy of the Bible.

There was outrage from some clerics when she addressed my church in May 1988 and used the scriptures to defend Thatcherism. In that speech she spoke of her own personal belief in the relevance of Christianity to public policy. Her quotations from the Bible were: 'If a man will not work he shall not eat' (St Paul to the Thessalonians); 'Thou shalt not covet' (the Tenth Commandment). Anyone who neglects to provide for his own house has disowned the faith and is 'worse than an infidel' (St Paul to Timothy). As for the biblical injunction to love our neighbour as ourselves, Margaret Thatcher chose the C. S. Lewis interpretation of it which, she said, *can* include hatred of our neighbour because sometimes, when we fall below the standards and beliefs we have accepted, we can hate even ourselves for an unworthy deed.

The furore that followed her address seemed to leave an impression that her linking of the scriptures with Thatcherism was something new, a recent invention designed to give a moral and religious credibility to her beliefs. Far from it. Not only was she born, brought up and married as a Methodist, but early in her Premiership, in May 1981, she delivered a highly significant speech at London's St Lawrence Jewry. While skilfully avoiding political issues in that speech, its contents amounted to a moral and religious philosophy. It showed that, for her, the foundations of Thatcherism are to be found in deeply held and tightly argued moral and religious beliefs. These beliefs are cemented together in

Britain by something that goes, in one sense, deeper than morality and religion: the instincts of the nation itself – a sense of justice and injustice and of the need to work for its own sake.

She set out in considerable detail in her St Lawrence speech how these beliefs and instincts intertwine through Thatcherism, and she emphasised that all responsibilities lie with the individual, not the State. She said:

> Of course, we can deduce from the teachings of the Bible principles of public as well as private morality. But, in the last resort, all these principles refer back to the individual in his relationship to others. We must always beware of supposing that somehow we can get rid of our own moral duties by handing them over to the community; that somehow we can get rid of our own guilt by talking about 'national' or 'social' guilt. We are called on to repent our own sins, not each other's sins.

She believes that all communities, held together by mutual dependence, need rules.

> They all need rules to enable them to live together harmoniously, and the rules must be backed by some kind of authority, however gently and subtly exercised. The nation is but an enlarged family. Because of its traditions, and the mutual love and loyalty which bind its members together, it should ideally need little enforcement to maintain its life. But alas, because of man's imperfections, evil is ever present, and the innocent must be protected from its ravages.

What followed from this, she said, was in a sense the most important point she had to make.

> We must never think of individual freedom and the social good as being opposed to each other. We must never suppose that where personal liberty is strong, society will be weak and impoverished, or that where the nation is strong the individual will necessarily be in shackles.
>
> The wealth of nations, the defence of national freedom and the well-being of society, all these depend on the faith and exertions of

men and women. It is an old and simple truth, but it is sometimes forgotten in political debate.

She is also insistent that, though Britain is now a so-called 'pluralist society' in which many different traditions of belief exist alongside each other, we remain a Christian nation. Even though there are what she herself described in that speech as 'considerable religious minorities' in Britain, the nation remains 'founded on biblical principles'.

One of Margaret Thatcher's strongest convictions is a belief in the British sense of fair play. For her, this is summed up by her favourite poem from Rudyard Kipling, 'Norman and Saxon', which she quoted in full at St Lawrence of Jewry, explaining:

> This sense of fair play is based on the acceptance by the majority in the nation of some moral absolutes which underpin our social and commercial relationships. In other words, we believe that just as there are physical laws which we break at our peril, so there are moral laws which, if we flout them, will lead to personal and national decline.
>
> If we as a nation had accepted, for instance, that violence, stealing and deception were plausible activities, then our moral fibre would soon have disintegrated.'

Another characteristic of the British nation is the sense that work is not only a necessity, it is a duty, and indeed a virtue: the work ethic.

> It is an expression of our dependence on each other. Work is not merely a way of receiving a pay packet but a means whereby everyone in the community benefits and society is enriched. Creating wealth must be seen as a Christian obligation if we are to fulfil our role as stewards of the resources and talents the Creator has provided for us.
>
> These characteristics of our nation, the acknowledgement of the Almighty, a sense of tolerance, an acknowledgement of moral absolutes and a positive view of work, have sustained us in the past.

She saw years of socialism as a threat to the nation's character, and believes that each generation must renew its spirit again if the integrity of the nation is to survive. When only a minority of people acknowledge the authority of God in their lives, people turn to the State to do so many things which in the past were the prerogative of the family.

Thatcherism holds that Britain must always have a 'national purpose' and that without it the gap is filled by the terrorism of the few and the 'eat, drink and be merry, for tomorrow we die' philosophy of others. In turn, this results in the grasping of wealth for its own sake and the pursuit of selfish pleasure. This national purpose, which needs to be established in the minds of young and old alike and renewed with each generation, must include the defence of values.

All her objectives depend for their achievement on the faith and the work of individuals. In turn, that brings her argument back to where Margaret Thatcher believes it begins: individual responsibility. I therefore make no apology for quoting again her St Lawrence of Jewry speech.

The State cannot create wealth. That depends on the exertions of countless people motivated not only by the wholesome desire to provide for themselves and their families, but also by a passion for excellence and a genuine spirit of public service.

The State cannot generate compassion; it can and must provide a 'safety net' for those who, through no fault of their own, are unable to cope on their own. There is need for far more generosity in our national life, but generosity is born in the hearts of men and women; it cannot be manufactured by politicians, and assuredly it will not flourish if politicians foster the illusion that the exercise of compassion can be left to officials. And so it is on the individual that the health of both Church and State depends.

Perhaps we have lost the idea that is inherent in Christ's parable of the talents. The steward who simply did not use the resources entrusted to him was roundly condemned. The two who used them to produce more wealth were congratulated and given more. To put up with the mediocre, to flinch from the challenge, to mutter 'the Government ought to be doing something about it', is not the way to rekindle the spirit of the nation.

And so what should we conclude about the relationship between the individual and the nation? I make no secret of my wish that everyone should be proud of belonging to this country. We have a past which, by any standard, is impressive; much in our present life and culture, too, commands great respect. We have as a nation a sense of perspective and a sense of humour; our scholars win international acclaim, our armed forces are renowned for their bravery and restraint, and our industries continue to do well in the markets of the world.

I want us to be proud of our nation for another reason. In the comity of nations, only a minority have a system of government which can be described as democratic. In these, economic and cultural life flourish because of the freedom their people enjoy. But a democratic system of government cannot be transferred to other nations simply by setting up imitations of our institutions – we have realised this all too clearly in recent times. For democracy to work, it requires what Montesquieu described as a special quality in the people: virtue, and I would add understanding. I believe this quality of virtue to be that derived from the biblical principles on which this nation, and the United States, among others, are founded.

I want this nation to continue to be heard in the world and for the leaders of other countries to know that our strength comes from shared convictions as to what is right and wrong and that we value the convictions enough to defend them.

The values which sustain our way of life have by no means dis-appeared, but they are in danger of being undermined. I believe we are able to generate the will and purpose to revive and maintain them.

This is summed up in a sermon by John Newton: 'Though the island of Great Britain exhibits but a small spot upon a map of the globe, it makes a splendid appearance in the history of mankind, and for a long space of time has been signally under the protection of God and a seat of peace, liberty and truth.'

'As Alastair Burnet intoned to television viewers with his huge gravitas that Margaret Thatcher was now back in Downing Street for the second time in succession, she leaned forward to stamp her feet and shout at his face on the screen: "I'm not! I'm not! I'm still here in Hendon Town Hall!"'

6

FIGHTING ELECTIONS

As HAS BEEN mentioned, Margaret Thatcher is in some ways a
superstitious Prime Minister, though the scientist in her would
deny it. She is, of course, extremely determined, and never more
so than in keeping the practices, precedents and traditions of her
work in Finchley exactly as they have been since she first arrived
there in 1959. But during General Elections she can make certain
decisions which may not be considered as having been influenced
by shrewd judgement alone. The spring is her favourite time for
elections, and in 1983 she began her campaign in East Finchley. It
did not seem to me to be a good place to start, given that Conservative support is not as great there as in other areas of the constituency, but she refused to be budged.

Her conviction that East Finchley was the place to start became
apparent as she stood in front of the log fire at Chequers the
evening before Cabinet Ministers arrived to discuss plans for the
General Election. It was just before midnight and the Prime
Minister had thrown a fresh log into the dying embers when she
began one of her long speeches, clearly directed neither at Ron
Thurlow, the Finchley Conservative Chairman, nor at me – though
we were the only others present in the room. She is prone to such
soliloquies, and it rapidly becomes clear to her small audience that

she is talking not to them but to herself. On this occasion she stood looking into the strengthening flames and recited her entire election campaign engagements, beginning with East Finchley and progressing through her *Panorama* appearance to her mid-campaign flight to Williamsburg for the world economic summit. To accentuate the point, she said: 'This is my eighth campaign, and I always start in East Finchley.'

Even the most rational of politicians can become superstitious at elections, with 'lucky' times and 'lucky' places. Certainly, May and June have proved to be Margaret Thatcher's time for winning General Elections. But whatever the reason that lay behind her decision of venue, East Finchley still did not seem to me to be the most propitious spot from which to launch her campaign; a more staunchly Conservative part of the constituency would have been preferable.

Undeterred, she arrived in East Finchley on the first Saturday of the election campaign, and once the media knew she was going to be there, about 400 writers, photographers, broadcasters and technicians descended. What happened next was blamed by the British television crews on their French colleagues. The French in turn blamed the Germans and, when asked, the Germans said it was all the fault of the Italians. Whoever was responsible, the butter counter in the supermarket in which the Prime Minister was appearing that morning was smashed in the media stampede. The evidence left behind indicated that some of the photographers had become so enthusiastic that they had stood inside the freezer compartments. To make matters worse, as she left the shop the Labour Party were out in force, as was perhaps to be expected in this part of the constituency. It was visible confirmation of my worse fears. The ensuing melee of shouting, heckling and booing was not the best background for the launching of the Prime Minister's campaign, and it was recorded with relish by the television crews.

In her diary of the 1983 election campaign, Carol Thatcher wrote that when her mother got back to the Finchley Conservative Association offices after this inauspicious start, she was not pleased. That was something of an understatement. That lunch-time, Margaret Thatcher marched into the office followed by Carol, Derek Howe, one of the press aides from Conservative Central Office, and me and demanded to know just how bad it was all going to look on the television screens that night. This, she declared, was the first day of the campaign and the British were going to see her being booed in her own constituency. For two minutes she told me in a variety of different ways that it was a total disgrace. Apparently my complexion paled, and I certainly remember feeling nauseous. Carol tried to be helpful; she said that most of the cameras were foreign, so it would not really matter. But this only served to inflame the Prime Minister again, this time at the humiliation of foreigners seeing her being booed in her own back yard.

Then Derek Howe decided on a different tactic. Confident in the knowledge that it was not he who had suggested that the campaign be launched in East Finchley, he asked in what appeared to be total innocence: 'Who on earth decided to start off there anyway?' There seemed to be nothing to lose as the room fell silent awaiting the response to his question, so I said: 'The candidate'. It was one of very few occasions when she was described by me as 'the candidate' and there was a pause while the room waited for the explosion. Instead, Margaret, with a generosity of spirit which I did not find unusual, rose to her feet, put her hand on my arm and said: 'Let's go for lunch. It's always like this on the first day.'

If the campaign got off to a bad start in Finchley, the run-up to nominations had promised to be disastrous. On 20 May I had been phoned by Dennis Signy, editor of the *Hendon and Finchley Times* and a good friend to Margaret Thatcher, the Conservative Party and myself, to alert me that a pseudo 'Margaret Thatcher' was going to stand for Parliament in Finchley. Thanks to his warning, I was at Hendon town hall on the following Monday when this other 'Margaret Thatcher' handed in his nomination papers. It would have been hilarious, save for the fact that this dark-bearded black man who had changed his name by deed poll was threatening to sabotage the Prime Minister's entire election campaign in Finchley.

[75]

His papers read: 'Margaret Thatcher, Conservation Party'. His agent was named as 'Ronald Reagan'. My efforts to get 'Margaret Thatcher' to tell me what his name had been before he changed it were fruitless. (Eventually, it transpired that his name had been Colin Hanoman.)

In the interval since Dennis Signy's phone call I had taken the opportunity to research electoral law, and I asked Signy to challenge Colin Hanoman with the fact that under a 1946 legal case he could not change his *christian* name by deed poll. Hanoman replied: 'My advisers, the National Council for Civil Liberties, have said that because I am not a practising Christian that does not apply to me.'

It appeared that the threat to the Prime Minister was serious. At the town hall I asked if Michael Bennett, the Acting Returning Officer for the election who was also Chief Executive and Town Clerk of Barnet, would invalidate the bearded 'Margaret Thatcher's' nomination papers. To help matters along, I said I would put in an objection. To do this two grounds are available: firstly, that the candidate's particulars are not as required by law; secondly, that the candidate's nomination paper is not as required by law. Against the precedent of a case in 1946, I entered an objection on the grounds that the bearded 'Margaret Thatcher's' nomination was an 'obvious unreality'. This was based on the fact that this 'Margaret Thatcher' was clearly male, and also that his election agent was one 'Ronald Reagan' – formerly Simon Stansfield until he, too, experienced an overwhelming desire for a world leader's name.

The closing moment for decisions was fast approaching. The next day I was asked to go back to the town hall to see Michael Bennett. He told me that he had not made up his mind whether or not to invalidate 'Margaret Thatcher's' nomination papers and was taking counsel's advice. He asked me if I realised the consequences of what was happening. If the other 'Margaret Thatcher's' nomination papers were invalidated, but subsequently after the General Election the High Court sustained an objection by him, then the poll in Finchley and Friern Barnet would be declared void. It would not be just that Finchley and Friern Barnet would not have a Member of Parliament. Even more importantly, the country would be left without a Prime Minister for some time. I replied that Sir Alec Douglas Home had not held a seat in the Commons for some weeks after he became Conservative Party Leader, but had nevertheless been Prime Minister. Michael Bennett simply repeated that I had to realise the consequences of my actions. Though I insisted that I did indeed realise those consequences, the comparison with Sir Alec Douglas Home was largely invalid, since he had been in the House of Lords when he became Conservative Party Leader, which was where in earlier decades many of our Prime Ministers had remained throughout their tenure of the office. In the scenario Michael Bennett was describing, Margaret Thatcher would be unable to gain access to either House except as a visitor. The constitutional crisis, not to mention the havoc that a Labour Opposition could wreak with it, was scarcely imaginable.

The following day, Michael Bennett told me that he had decided to invalidate Hanoman's nomination papers. But the real Margaret Thatcher's problems were only just beginning. For the black and bearded version was off to the Royal Courts of Justice in London's Strand to appeal against this decision.

Throughout this episode my conversations with the Prime Minister were brief and formal. In this case, being a lawyer herself, she wanted to deal with the legal officials – initially David Mitchell, the legal officer at Conservative Central Office, who in one day alone was seven times involved in separate discussions with her on the legal technicalities. He warned her that large teams of lawyers and a substantial sum of money would be involved. She fielded a QC and two junior barristers. David Mitchell also warned her that winning in the High Court and, if necessary, at appeal would not automatically mean that the other 'Margaret Thatcher' or the National Council for Civil Liberties would pick up the costs. Nor could Conservative Central Office assist financially.

It was a bizarre experience sitting in the Royal Courts of Justice watching the bearded 'Margaret Thatcher' claim that his Conservation Party was being denied an opportunity to field him in

Finchley when the Loony Party, Anti-Censor and Ban Every Licensing Law Society were getting a chance to put up candidates against the Prime Minister. Indeed, according to his evidence, in other constituencies parties which were being given the chance to field candidates included the Freddies' Alternative Medicine Party, the Fancy Dress Party, the Loony Monster Green Chicken Alliance, the Nobody Party and the Traditional English Food Party. Interestingly, both Colin Hanoman and Simon Stansfield (as they once had been) were seen by their deed polls to have changed their names on the same day, 20 May 1983.

The real Margaret Thatcher won in the High Court, but by then the contest was entirely in the hands of the legal profession so, although it looked to be all over, the court rose and effectively moved next door for an appeal by the bearded 'Margaret Thatcher' who, whatever else he was, certainly was tenacious and not short of a bob or two. The real version won again, and only then could we march across the zebra crossing at London's Strand and into the Wig and Pen club for champagne – the election campaign could at last really get under way. However, there may not have been quite such a vigorous popping of corks in the flat over 10 Downing Street that evening as there was among the barristers and solicitors in the Wig and Pen. Someone had to pay a massive legal bill, and, though there is no definitive evidence to hand, my suspicion has always been that a very real bill was picked up by the real Denis Thatcher.

A month later, when Margaret Thatcher was reinstated in 10 Downing Street with a landslide majority of 144, she sent me a charming letter of thanks for my help, written in her own beautifully flowing hand. It concluded with the slightest of stings in its tail. She remarked that we really must ensure a more efficient count on polling night at the next General Election. Behind that exhortation lay events known to few outside her immediate circle on the night of the 1983 count, but which reveal a side to the Prime Minister that is rarely seen by the public.

The physical problems of counting the votes in Hendon town hall on the night of 9 June 1983 and through into the early hours of 10 June stemmed from the fact that three constituencies other than

Finchley and Friern Barnet were also being counted there: Hendon North, Hendon South and Chipping Barnet. Carol Thatcher in her diary recalls merely that the count went 'on and on'. It certainly did for Margaret Thatcher and Finchley and Friern Barnet, although not for the other three constituencies.

For security reasons Margaret, Denis, Carol and Mark Thatcher were kept in a side room off the main counting area, and to keep them abreast of developments throughout the country was a television tuned to Independent Television and Alastair Burnet, the Prime Minister's favourite combination on such occasions. With Margaret Thatcher and her family was David Boddy, the former Director of Press and Public Relations at Conservative Central Office who had left to start his own public affairs consultancy but who had been called back by the Prime Minister to help her avoid incidents such as that early in the campaign which had left a trail of destruction in the East Finchley supermarket.

I often left the floor where the votes were being counted and popped into the side room to give a progress report to Margaret Thatcher. Each time I went in to her she was angrier than the last. The reason for this was that Michael Bennett, the Acting Returning Officer, had decided, because of the importance of the Finchley and Friern Barnet result, to deal with this separately and had therefore arranged to have the ballot papers of the other three constituencies counted first.

At 1.30 a.m. Alastair Burnet was forecasting that Margaret Thatcher would again be Prime Minister, because the Conservatives were set for a majority of seats in the Commons. By this time, she was threatening to leave her room and 'go out there and find out just what's going on'. I was becoming desperate. Leaving the room to return to the count, I spotted John Gorst, the successful Conservative candidate in Hendon North, coming down the corridor, and after a swift explanation that the family were having trouble stopping the Prime Minister from going on the rampage, I bundled him into the room to help relieve the tension.

At 1.50 a.m. I called back to bring Margaret Thatcher up to date on the snail-like progress of her count. On the television screen in front of her, Alastair Burnet was declaring with his huge gravitas that this was the moment that the Conservatives had reached the magic figure of seats won. The Conservatives had an overall majority of seats in the House of Commons and Margaret Thatcher was Prime Minister for the second term in succession. He intoned to the watching world: 'She is back in Downing Street.' What he did not realise, and nor did the millions of viewers, was that as he was speaking on the screen, Margaret Thatcher was leaning forward in her chair to stamp her feet and shout at the screen: 'I'm not! I'm not! I'm still here in Hendon Town Hall!'

Finally, at just before 2.30 a.m., Margaret Thatcher adjusted her make-up and her fury and walked out into the hall to receive the news that she had been duly elected as the Member of Parliament for Finchley and Friern Barnet. That night and early morning in Hendon town hall there was clearly something amiss that went beyond her feelings about organisation at her count. The final opinion polls were pointing to a landslide for her, and her mood should have been one of undisguised satisfaction. The clue to her mood lay in an unexpected change to her programme for the constituency on polling day. She had been due to stay there from 10.30 a.m. to 4 p.m., but left instead at around 3 p.m. to return to Conservative Central Office. She had gone to see Cecil Parkinson, then Party Chairman, and he had broken the news of his affair. In my view, he might perhaps have waited a little longer before taking the shine off that day and its famous victory.

Margaret is usually highly self-disciplined and controls any irritability she may be feeling, always falling back on one of Alderman Roberts' favourite maxims that there is nothing that can be done about milk that is spilled. But her anger broke through that night, as it had done during her first General Election campaign as Opposition Leader when, in the last throes of the campaign with victory looking less than secure, it was suggested that she should call in Edward Heath to appear with her in the final Party Election Broadcast on television, an event which tradition and plain common sense dictates should be monopolised by the Party Leader. No one around her at the time will own up to being responsible for the suggestion – though responsibility has been laid at second hand on Lord Thorneycroft, then Party Chairman – but the reaction it received is vividly recalled. She went white with fury and stormed out of the room. Denis Thatcher said he had never seen her so upset.

The 1987 General Election was entirely different. It was as if that irritability which had burst out in the early hours at Hendon town hall had returned to permeate the entire campaign. The tensions and arguments between Margaret Thatcher and Norman Tebbit, at that time Party Chairman, in the run-up to the election have been well documented. What is not generally known is that in February 1987, four months before she called the General Election, Margaret Thatcher carried out a surprisingly candid examination of her own public image.

The 'image' problem had first been identified in April 1986 when she met at Chequers with Norman Tebbit, his Chief of Staff Michael Dobbs, and others engaged in the long-term planning for what was to become the 1987 General Election. It was then that Margaret Thatcher learned the existence of the initials TBW, and what they stood for: That Bloody Woman. With such forth-rightness were the differing perceptions of the Prime Minister laid bare that she became aware of the antagonism towards her from some quarters. According to one account, the meeting ended with her becoming suspicious that Norman Tebbit was trying to indicate that the only thing that stood in the way of a third successive Conservative win was her as Prime Minister and that she should make way for him. If this was her suspicion, however unjustified, then it accounts for much of the deteriorating relationship between the two in the months that followed.

Margaret Thatcher decided to tackle, in her own way, the problem of her image. She called in a specialist adviser on women's images to discuss her clothes and general presentation. It may be that this ability to be objective about self-presentation is a trait that is stronger in women than men. The adviser, who deals with individuals in the same way that other consultancies deal with companies, must have been as flattered as she was surprised. To my knowledge, not only had she never met Margaret Thatcher before but had had no connection with the Conservative Party. Just where the Prime Minister heard her name is not clear, but the decision to invite her in appears to have been hers alone. Margaret Thatcher asked her what she was doing wrong. Much of the discussion centred on clothes, and shortly afterwards an executive from Aquascutum was called in to help to create a new-look Margaret Thatcher. Out went those matronly outfits and fussy bows at the neck, and in came a new wardrobe of well-styled suits with fashionable shoulders and a square-cut look. The colours of her clothes also changed. The blues became darker and stronger and her wardrobe filled with checks of black and white and grey and white.

The timetable for launching the new image was set. It would first be tried out on Mikhail Gorbachev during her visit to Moscow in March 1987, and then on the British electorate. The change was sufficiently stunning to provoke the desired comments when she went to Russia, and to propel her into her third election campaign. It also did much to bolster her spirits and confidence.

While the ensuing electoral victory with a majority of 101 was more than satisfactory, the campaign was marred by Norman Tebbit falling at the first fence upon his appointment as Party Chairman by Margaret Thatcher. The first rule of his predecessor Cecil Parkinson in the run-up to the 1983 poll had been to ensure that at every stage the Prime Minister was satisfied and happy. He had argued, sensibly, that everything and everyone would fall into place if this cardinal rule were maintained. But things did not run so smoothly in 1987, and can be summed up by one incident out on the campaign trail.

In the countryside and half-way across a field, Margaret Thatcher declared that she wanted to address some distant onlookers of the non-media variety. 'Fetch a megaphone,' she ordered. To the immense credit of the Central Office team also in the middle of the field, a megaphone was produced, albeit of the type that seemed to have provided best service between the wars. Grasping the megaphone in one hand ready to speak, she then thrust it back at her entourage and snapped rattily: 'I can't be seen with a megaphone. This is ridiculous.'

Though Norman Tebbit was blamed for so much of the bad feeling that ran through the run-up to the campaign, as well as the days on the hustings, there was one other personal reason why Margaret Thatcher was not in the best of spirits in the first days after the election was called: a painful abscess under a tooth.

In Finchley, however, she remained serene and less nervous than she had been in 1983. A number of journalists phoned me to ask how the problems at Central Office were affecting the Prime Minister in her constituency. It was not necessary to find a diplomatic reply. The truth was that she seemed happier and more at home than usual. If there were crises in Smith Square, she left them there when she crossed the North Circular Road into Finchley. Her constituency has always been something of a relaxation for her. During those three weeks, it became nothing short of a refuge. She was home with her Finchley family.

'In my diary are three dates – my annual meeting, Finchley Carnival and the Christmas party down on the Grange Estate – and if President Reagan or Foreign Ministers want to see me they know now they can find me in Finchley.'

(Margaret Thatcher)

7

THE MEMBER OF PARLIAMENT
FOR FINCHLEY

To MARGARET THATCHER, the people of her north London constituency are a second family. She may be Prime Minister, but in
practice she cannot continue so for long unless she has a seat in the
Commons. Finchley and Friern Barnet gives her that seat but it also
gives her so much more, which helps to explain her description of
it as her 'Finchley family'.

Within the Government in the United Kingdom, there are two
types of Minister. One has a constituency to which he or she is
answerable every four years or so at a General Election – a collec-
tion of about 80,000 voters who collectively, like Caesar in the
Colosseum in Rome, turn their thumb up or down and thus give
political life or death. The second type of Minister has no constituency, sits in the House of Lords and so far as the practice of
government is concerned is equal in status and rank to those who
are MPs. But in the real world of Westminster politics, the
Ministers without constituencies are regarded as inferior. They
have the advantage of no daily postbag from constituents, no
burdensome visits to constituency surgeries, no summer garden
parties and Christmas fêtes to open. But they suffer from the
disadvantage that they have no political roots. They do not get a
sense of what troubles voters, because there are no ebbs and flows

in their postbags, no surge of complaints at constituency surgeries, no warmth or chill to experience on the pavements and doorsteps.

It is one of the marvels of the unwritten constitution of Britain that the Prime Minister, like every other Minister and MP, also has to deal with a constituency. What is even more remarkable is that this contact with the ordinary voters, on whom the Prime Minister of the day depends for ultimate political survival, continues daily through 10 Downing Street itself. Thus, within four hours every working morning at Number 10, Margaret Thatcher has essentially three different roles.

6 a.m.–9 a.m.   Margaret Thatcher, housewife and citizen, rises and prepares breakfast for Denis, reads the newspapers and listens to the radio – unfailingly BBC Radio Four's *Today* programme.

9 a.m.–10 a.m.   Margaret Thatcher, MP for Finchley, goes down one floor from the flat to a one-roomed constituency office manned by Joy Robilliard, her constituency secretary. Into this room every week over 300 letters arrive from the constituency and all which relate in any way to Finchley are seen by Margaret Thatcher and dealt with according to her instructions. Every letter is signed by her.

10 a.m.   Margaret Thatcher, Prime Minister of Great Britain and Northern Ireland, descends one more flight of stairs to take up her duties in her office on the first floor.

Below is the Cabinet Room which she attends every Thursday when the Commons is sitting, for a meeting of the full Cabinet. It is used on many other days, too, for smaller meetings of Ministers. Sometimes she simply prefers to work there. The Cabinet Room is a very special place, not just because of the decisions that have been and will be made there, but because it is electronically protected to prevent prying, spying ears from hearing what is said. Take a pocket tape recorder into the Cabinet Room and you will leave with nothing but a scramble of electronic mush on the tape.

It's great news – Margaret Thatcher carries her message to the electors of North Finchley

Margaret Thatcher, looking out from her father's shop window, helps to win the seat for a fellow candidate in the 1979 General Election

World Leaders have to wait as Margaret Thatcher puts on a glamorous dress for the Grange Estate Old Folks Party in Finchley

Yes, she does listen!

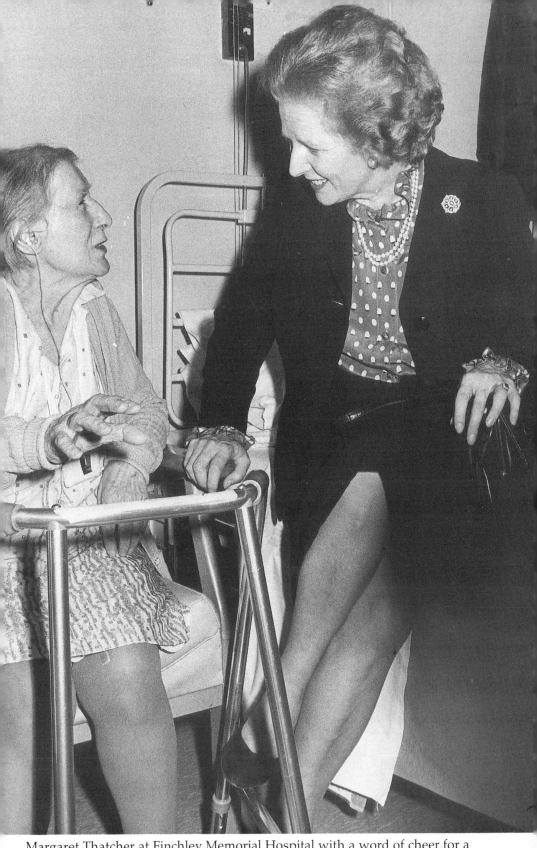

Margaret Thatcher at Finchley Memorial Hospital with a word of cheer for a patient

Marmalade for Denis and tea towels for Chequers at the Finchley Christmas Fair – as the author waits patiently

Margaret Roberts' teddy bear helping to raise funds for charity

'The Winning Team' after the 1983 Finchley election result

Agent and candidate working together for victory in the 1987 General Election

Margaret Thatcher with members of her 'fan club'

12.30 or 1 p.m. Sometimes official business or State lunches for Margaret Thatcher, usually on Monday and Wednesday, and sandwiches and coffee or a light snack lunch on Tuesdays and Thursdays as she prepares for the twice-weekly fifteen minutes of Prime Minister's Question Time. She takes the pre-Question Time briefing very seriously, and her political and Civil Service aides will seek to prime and prepare her for every conceivable question that the Leader of the Opposition and other MPs might throw at her. Performing well at Question Time is vitally important. Westminster is a jungle, the Prime Minister is king of the jungle, and if performance is seen to flag then the predators on both sides start jostling ready for the kill.

Her Fridays are divided up neatly each month. So in every four weeks she spends two Fridays as Prime Minister, one Friday as Leader of the Conservative Party and/or Prime Minister visiting every part of the United Kingdom, and one Friday in Finchley as its Member of Parliament.

Her Friday in Finchley will begin, as usual, in the flat at the top of 10 Downing Street. It will be followed by the regular call to her constituency office in the floor below before she goes down to the Prime Minister's office for an hour or so before departing for Finchley. What lies ahead in less than a day in Finchley are events that will result in her meeting as many as 800 people, making five speeches and eating anything from caviar to steak and kidney pudding.

A typical working day in Finchley begins with departure at noon from Number 10 with a 'Garden Girl' secretary (so called because the office this cluster of super secretaries work in looks out on the Downing Street garden) and her Finchley file containing her timetable and briefing notes on her engagements. A fairly standard engagement would be a lunch-time meeting with businessmen and representatives of other groups at Hendon Hall Hotel. Such gatherings are arranged about three times a year and apart from local businessmen, others attending could include a doctor, a headmistress and a local newspaper photographer to record the events for the local press.

Other rigidly fixed engagements in her political diary in Finchley will include the Conservative Association's annual dinner dance at the beginning of the year, its Annual General Meeting in the spring, a party for Association members in May, the Ladies' Lunch in October, and Christmas Fair in the autumn. Other non-political but equally fixed engagements include the summer Finchley Carnival and a visit to a pensioners' Christmas party in December – an event she has attended without a break since 1959. When her Finchley family celebrated her twenty-five years as their MP with a party for 300, she told them: 'In my diary are three dates – my annual meeting, Finchley Carnival and the Christmas party down on the Grange Estate – and if President Reagan or Foreign Ministers want to see me they know now they can find me in Finchley.'

The first lunch-time function on a Friday in Finchley will follow a standard pattern which is to her liking: a plain meal served efficiently and taking fifty minutes. She will then speak for up to twenty-five minutes, and fifteen minutes of question time will end the lunch. On these occasions, the trouble would begin when I tried to ensure her prompt departure. Everyone wants to talk with her, shake her hand on the way out and generally delay the timetable. Yet the next engagement is likely to be at a primary school where Margaret Thatcher has in advance set down strict instructions. 'There must be no delays,' she insists, 'so the parents can collect their children when they expect to do so.' But the most likely cause of any delay will be Margaret herself when she meets the children. A stickler for punctuality and efficiently run programmes, the most carefully arranged timetable will go awry when she and small children are put together. The afternoon event will usually run for about an hour and will end with a cup of tea with staff and parents, a short speech and a final farewell to the ladies in the kitchen – a courtesy she never forgets at any function, big or small.

The next stop on a typical Friday could be the Finchley Memorial Hospital, a small cottage hospital in the heart of her constituency with which Margaret has had a long association. She turned a sod at the start of the extension to the Elderly Persons' Day Centre, and was back fourteen months later to open it, chat to the old folk, some of whom she knows, and to talk with staff, doctors and members of the Area and District Health Boards. On visits to the hospital she will make a speech, unveil a plaque, have a cup of tea and break off to talk with ambulance men and women on the way out. The engagement takes about an hour, and afterwards she will go back to the Finchley Conservative Association office at Ballards Lane where she will have another cup of tea, this time with the agent, and discuss anything connected with the constituency, from a deputation she is to meet later in the day to next month's programme of engagements.

At 5.15 p.m. precisely the first constituent will come through the door into the office for her constituency surgery. She insists on punctuality, saying: 'We mustn't keep them waiting. Who's first?' Much of the constituency work can and is done by post, but there is some that has to be done face to face, such as meeting deputations of constituents from, say, the National Union of Teachers, or local dentists. The timetable target says that she should have finished her surgery by 6.20 p.m., but she will probably over-run after promising her constituents to raise particular problems with Government Departments and then to write to them with the results of her enquiries.

At 6.40 p.m., twenty minutes later than her timetable, she will go upstairs for a whisky and soda, with salad or shepherd's pie prepared by Tessa Phillips, the office secretary. The same meal goes to all the Special Branch and other 10 Downing Street staff who have travelled with her to Finchley. If Margaret is not overloaded with paperwork or phone calls to handle in the downstairs office, she will want to eat upstairs with everyone else rather than work on alone. Sometimes this is impossible, because during her constituency surgery 10 Downing Street will have been on the phone to its Garden Girl secretary travelling with her, and there is often urgent Government business for her to attend to over the telephone.

At 7.30 p.m. she will leave the constituency office for a round of engagements, often Conservative Association visits arranged around its branches. Ten minutes later she will be at the first function, attended by perhaps 250 people sitting at eight or ten separate tables. She will walk around each table and be able to recognise almost everyone by name. They will be fairly representative of her constituency – some young marrieds, a good number of pensioners, and sprinklings of Cypriots and Asians. At about 8.30 p.m. she will express her regret at having to leave, and make a short speech before departing ten minutes later for a second, almost identical function, save that by the time she arrives at about 8.50 p.m. this group of guests will have completed their main course. She may join them with a glass of wine or even a little pudding. Then she will make her final speech of the day, but usually it will not be a mere repetition of the polite one she made at the earlier dinner. By now, the end of the day will be approaching and she will have begun to assimilate it in her mind. This time the listeners are likely to be treated to fifteen minutes of what amounts to a combination of a 'state of the nation' and 'state of Finchley' speech. She will draw on her experiences of the day and what she has been told by businessmen, teachers, dentists and others. She will deftly weave together her experiences in Finchley since lunchtime. These short, off-the-cuff speeches are among the most remarkable I have ever heard in politics. Without speechwriters or teleprompt, Margaret Thatcher presents the work and ambitions of her Government. Then she sets off back to Number 10, usually with Denis Thatcher who will have caught up with her during the day's engagements.

The guests from that night's events will make their way home, most exhausted and many to explain to friends the next day that they are a little tired because they spent the previous evening at a Party function with their MP – the PM. But Margaret and Denis Thatcher will be heading southwards to the flat over 10 Downing Street where she will once more become Prime Minister. When the Conservatives in Finchley have long gone to bed, she will work through her boxes of Government papers until 1 a.m. or later. And, as her final speech of the day has shown, the woman sitting reading, ticking pages and writing notes in the margins of the documents is doing so not just as Prime Minister but also as the Member of Parliament for Finchley.

'Outside, in the United Kingdom and the world, she can wreak great changes. In Finchley Conservative Association, life goes on much as it always has.'

8

HER FINCHLEY FAMILY

IT TAKES forty-five minutes for Margaret Thatcher's black Daimler to drive from 10 Downing Street to Finchley. As the car crosses London's North Circular Road she enters her constituency, and as she does so she changes subtly. The Special Branch men who travel with her have noticed this change, and say that she seems to be taking off the role of Prime Minister and settling herself into the role of Member of Parliament.

There is a sameness about the north-west London suburb which can be slightly depressing to the newcomer. For Margaret, Finchley is a second home after Grantham and it is a repository of many of the same virtues that she found in her childhood home. In many respects, Finchley is for the Prime Minister what she feels the rest of the United Kingdom should be like.

At a personal level, the Finchley Conservative Association is a time capsule to which she returns, as she has since her adoption as candidate in 1959, to find that nothing much has really changed. In most London and suburban Conservative Associations there is a rapid and inevitable turnover of key officers. Not so in Finchley. There the continuity and the feeling that Finchley is unchanging is underpinned by many of the figures around her today. They have been there since the 'swinging sixties'. She calls them her 'Finchley family', and they have grown up together, like a family. Some of the key men and women in the Association today were the Young Conservatives who in 1959 voted for her as their candidate. The Association's President, Frank Gibson, was the constituency's Young Conservatives' Chairman at her selection meeting. Ron Thurlow, the Chairman today who guided the constituency through the 1983 and 1987 General Elections, also voted for Margaret Thatcher on what proved to be an historic occasion in 1959.

That sense of other-worldliness about the Finchley Conservative Association was sensed and summed up by Dennis Signy, editor of the *Hendon and Finchley Times*, during the Westland crisis in 1986 which cost Margaret Thatcher two of her Cabinet Ministers – first Michael Heseltine then Leon Brittan. Signy, observing the events in Finchley on the Saturday after Leon Brittan quit, and before the censure debate in the Commons on the Monday, wrote: 'There are times in the life of even the most cynical and hard-bitten journalist when the feeling arises that Finchley and environs is cut off from the rest of the country by a Hadrian's Wall.'

What Dennis Signy could not record was that on the following Monday, just hours before Labour launched its censure debate and saw it turned into a political damp squib by its leader, Neil Kinnock, Margaret Thatcher told Viscount Whitelaw, then her deputy, that she might no longer be Prime Minister that evening. In short, she feared she was about to lose the confidence of her Conservative back-bench MPs.

Signy did, however, record the scene in the Selborne Hall at Southgate that Saturday night.

And there was Mrs Thatcher, in the less exacting role of the MP for Finchley and Friern Barnet, in a long black-frilled evening gown with short velvet jacket, socialising with some 200 constituents, sipping a scotch, dancing with husband Denis to the music of the Contrasts . . . and seemingly without a care in the world.

Crisis? What crisis? Is the rest of the country, in the words of the rookie soldier who got a rocket from the drill sergeant, out of step with Finchley? Or is this a Tory dreamland?

[96]

He also recorded, with total accuracy, that her Conservatives gave her two standing ovations that night instead of the customary one, and that when Constituency Chairman Ron Thurlow declared that everyone was bored with Westland, the resonant voice of Denis Thatcher could be heard above the round of cheers and 'hear hears'.

It was not so much the dreamlike quality of the Finchley Conservative Association that struck me when I first arrived there to start work for Margaret Thatcher, as its immense conservatism. It was a conservatism that seemed out of place in the Britain that Margaret Thatcher was seeking to build. In 10 Downing Street she is the most revolutionary Conservative Prime Minister for a century. But as soon as she crosses the North Circular, she becomes in all matters relating to her Conservative Association the original stick-in-the-mud. Hardly any part of Britain's economic or social life has escaped her new broom; not so in the Finchley Association. Within days of taking over as her agent I designed a new, bold letter-head composed of white lettering on a solid Tory blue background. The title was bold and clear: 'Finchley Conservatives'. After all, that was what I thought we were. My initiative did not go down well with the officers of the Conservative Association, although that did not greatly surprise me. What did surprise me was the support they received from Margaret Thatcher. It was left to the new agent not only to retain the full and formal title, but to incorporate all nine words into it. The only concession to change was a colour photograph of the Member of Parliament, but that was hardly a radical move. By that time Margaret Thatcher had been the Finchley MP for twenty-two years.

My first visit to Finchley was one evening in January 1982 when I joined Margaret and Denis Thatcher for the Conservative Association's annual dinner. My journey there gave me time to reflect that my political inheritance as her agent was not one of great riches. At the previous General Election, that which had turned her from Leader of Her Majesty's Opposition into Prime Minister, the electorate of Finchley had rewarded her with a swing to the Conservatives of 4.7 per cent, lower than the London average. Her majority was 7878 over Labour, and though no one really thought that the Prime Minister's seat could fall to Labour at the subsequent General Election, the figures had an uncomfortable feel about them when, at this point in the life of the new Government, the Conservative line on the opinion polls' graphs seemed each week to find a new low point.

Subsequently, foreign journalists despatched to the Prime Minister's constituency were to explain to me that the very name of Finchley had seemed to them, before arriving, to have a certain ring of wealth and cushioned southern English suburban cosiness. Consequently, foreign journalists and I shared the same surprise at the reality of Finchley.

My inheritance contained a surprisingly high percentage of privately rented accommodation, over 20 per cent of the total. Over 16 per cent of the population was non-white, a figure that had doubled since the 1930s. Many of the non-whites were Asians, living mainly in wards such as East Finchley where Labour was the strongest party. It was Finchley itself and the separate community of Friern Barnet that were much more strongly Conservative. The Jewish community numbered 12,000–13,000 and divided into the industrious immigrant Jews with their market stalls and East European background, and the second-generation manufacturers with their penthouse flats in Regent's Park Road. The constituency has a false reputation for Jewish predominance. In fact there are nearly as many East Africans as Jews. For when Uganda's Idi Amin expelled 12,000 of them, many refugees settled in the constituency, bringing with them a primarily Conservative philosophy and a passion for hard work. To add the final cosmopolitan touch, there were several thousand Cypriots who had fled Cyprus when Turkey invaded their island in 1974.

There is not the slightest doubt that on occasions such as that when she spoke to the 'Refuseniks' in Russia during her visit there in 1987, and when she speaks of refugees and others fleeing persecution, Margaret Thatcher has in mind the many personal stories she has heard in her own constituency. These stories of persecution and escape from various repressive regimes have been a constant phenomenon throughout her years in Finchley, and she can explain in the smallest detail the history of the flood of Jewish refugees from Eastern Europe in 1922. She gave me a history lesson on refugees in 1982 when synagogues in Finchley commemorated that exodus on its sixtieth anniversary. It is hardly surprising, against the background of a constituency with so many immigrants, that Margaret Thatcher becomes a little impatient at the bi-annual Commonwealth Conference when Prime Ministers of countries such as Canada, Australia and New Zealand seek to lecture her about Britain's immigration rules.

What is so appealing to Margaret Thatcher is the love of hard work and sense of community and self-help displayed by many of these ethnic groupings. But the discovery of just how much she draws on her Finchley family was some way off when I first entered the public house reception room where the Conservative Association's annual dinner was taking place.

Just to describe that first evening as agent in Finchley says much about my subsequent six years there and about Margaret Thatcher's ultra-conservatism. My first thought on entering The Cherry Tree for the dinner was that the Conservative Association should consider a more upmarket venue the next year. But the annual dinner and dance has been held there since at least 1959 when Margaret Thatcher became MP, and the idea of a change is more than just unacceptable. Merely to suggest any change is to bring about the same reaction in Margaret Thatcher and her Association as she evoked in the Labour Party at the idea of selling off the nationalised industries. Outside, in the United Kingdom and the world, she can wreak great changes. In Finchley Conservative Association, life goes on much as it always has.

The programme for the dinner was clearly running late and John Tiplady, then the Constituency Chairman, asked Margaret and Denis if they would start the dancing. She said 'Yes, but then I'm going.' It sounded strange, almost extraordinary, that she was not going to stay, mingle and chat. Certainly, this was a contrast to the bright, bustling Prime Minister who had greeted and charmed me at Blackpool's Imperial Hotel. But in the intervening time, Margaret Thatcher had endured the anguish and stress of her son Mark getting himself lost, feared dead, for five days during a rally in the Sahara.

As the Prime Minister walked off the dance floor with Denis that night, apparently to go home, my rationalisation was that they were too exhausted for socialising. It was as they walked past the bar and towards the exit that she spotted four Conservative councillors from Barnet Council, on which Finchley representatives sit. One was the Conservative group leader, Councillor Leslie Pym. The effect on Margaret Thatcher was as if a large needle containing adrenalin had been inserted in a vein. She veered smartly away from both her husband and the exit to march up to Councillor Pym and demand: 'What are you doing about the rates this year, Leslie?' Thirty-five minutes later, a very angry Denis Thatcher was urging me: 'Go on – go in there and get her out, will you?' It seemed incautious to accept such an instruction on my first working day with the Prime Minister, especially in view of the verbal pasting Councillor Pym was getting. Friendly onlookers took me out of the hearing of Denis and advised me that my instinct for self-preservation was sound.

The experience was salutary. In the years that followed, I took care not to arrange a single meeting between Margaret Thatcher and the Conservative councillors on Barnet Council. For allowing her to sit round the same table would have ended with blood on the floor, and it would not have been hers. That they are Conservative councillors matters little to her. She cannot see a councillor, let alone a bunch of them, without the conviction rising rapidly in her that they could be running their council under a much stricter financial regime.

The effect on her of councillors and the question of local rates was to become predictable, although no less extraordinary for that. Some years later in Finchley she was chatting away happily during a reception at a bank when she spotted a notice on a far wall. Her face became worried and she broke away to walk over to examine it. It was a poster advertising the bank's home and contents insurance under a bold heading: 'Our Rates Are a Steal'. 'There you are,' she said with relief to the bank staff. 'I thought you were complaining about paying too much in local authority rates.'

The Conservative Association's annual general meeting provided yet further evidence of the personally conservative nature of this most radical of Prime Ministers. The meeting had always to be held in a local hall on the first Monday in the same month each year. Once I suggested to her that the ritual arrival at 7.55 p.m. for 8 p.m. be varied so that she could attend a major Jewish event at a local synagogue. A start thirty minutes later than had been the case since 1959 seemed reasonable for just one year. But she would have none of it, and instructed me to stick to precedent. The Jewish organisers had to rearrange their timetable to suit the routine of the Conservative Association.

Though the Jews in Finchley are not the largest identifiable group in numbers, their influence and cohesiveness is significant. In fact, after Margaret Thatcher arrived as MP in 1959 there was a fear that what seemed to be her safe Conservative seat could be lost because of the desertion of the Jewish vote. When anyone asked her about this at that time she would apparently reply: 'It's the golf club, you know. That's where it all started and where the whole thing has come from.' This was a reference to the alleged discrimination against them experienced by some Jews at the golf club, which refused membership to a number of applicants who wrote 'Jewish' in the column on the form marked 'Religion'. The result was that in the May 1963 local elections the Liberals polled 18,000 votes, 5000 more than the Conservatives.

The 'Jewishness' of the constituency has often been played up subsequently in the media, such as when the Prime Minister went to Israel and the appeasement of Jewish voters was said to be a reason. In reality, the influence of the Jewish vote is founded more on the prejudices of those who seek to make an issue of it. However, one scene remains vividly in my mind. It was when the Prime Minister attended a Jewish function shortly after she agreed in April 1986 to allow American bombers to fly from British bases against Libyan targets. As she walked in, there was weeping, wailing and a forest of hands reaching out to touch her. For a non-Jew, it was almost embarrassing. About 120 people were present and I struggled to make a space for her amid the grasping hands, for she intensely dislikes any crowding or threat of being crowded. But my efforts were useless. I was crushed, and the Special Branch officers were crushed too. When the chairman of the meeting declared that Margaret Thatcher stood firm against terrorism, the applause went on for minutes. It was equally prolonged when he declared that there had never been such a friend of Israel as Margaret Thatcher. She is held in high regard by the Jewish community, and on her sixtieth birthday 60 trees were planted by the Finchley Friends of Israel on the Golan Heights.

The strength she derives from her Finchley family comes not so much from any one group as from the totality of experience it gives her. Away from the cameras and microphones in Finchley, she will tell audiences and individuals that she travels abroad and works in 10 Downing Street as the MP for Finchley as well as in the role of British Prime Minister. A cynic might respond that she *would* say that, but, though she insists on the immutability of the rituals within her Conservative Association, she does draw deeply on the experiences and events in the constituency as catalysts for many of the changes which her Government has brought about. Two areas of Government policy – the abolition of local rates and of rent controls – have been embarked upon largely at her personal insistence and in great measure because of her experiences in Finchley.

Though she has nothing personally against the Conservative or other councillors in Finchley, it was clear from the moment that she engaged the luckless Councillor Pym in the bar at The Cherry Tree that she has an intense dislike for the power that councillors have over the level of local rates. At national level, the issue of the replacement of local rates was subjected to more discussion by the Cabinet and its committees than almost any other single domestic issue, and the outcome was always that there was no better way of raising the revenue than by local rates. In the end, it became a personal issue for Margaret Thatcher. She took the chair of the relevant Cabinet committee, pushed through her own proposal for a community charge, and won for herself the not entirely misplaced title of the only member of the Cabinet to support the change to the system. It does not take many months in her company to realise that she wants the new charge because she believes that it will result in more people telling the likes of Councillor Pym and his colleagues that they should spend less money.

In the case of both local rates and rent controls, she has been influenced greatly by the many old people living alone in Finchley. By 1982 many of the semi-detached houses in the constituency which had once been filled with families were occupied only by widows whose children had moved away. The character of parts of the constituency was clearly changing, and with this change came the need for new political solutions. It was a trip around some of these once prosperous 'semis' in 1982, organised by Finchley Old People's Welfare, that strengthened her determination to free up the rental market, so allowing large houses occupied by one person to be more easily occupied by tenants. The plight of all these old people with full local rates assessed on a house occupied only by themselves also encouraged her to press on with the idea that she was then developing for a community charge.

She has a possessiveness about Finchley which has strengthened rather than diminished under the national and international demands on her. More than once – but especially in April 1983 just before the General Election – there were rumours that a Gloucestershire Conservative MP with a rock-solid majority was going to stand down, and that Margaret Thatcher would take over his constituency. Chris Moncrieffe, the chief political correspondent of the Press Association, phoned me to ask if the stories were true. I told him the rumours were rubbish, but suggested that he should also ask 10 Downing Street. He did just that. The enquiry was given the serious attention that any from the country's premier news agency deserves, and therefore went all the way up the chain of command until it reached the Prime Minister. What was then transmitted back to Chris Moncrieffe was a straightforward denial; what he never knew was the effect of his enquiry upon her. The official whose task was to relay the question to her said: 'She went charging about, shouting and yelling.' For her, Finchley always comes first. Her loyalty to the constituency matches its loyalty to her.

Similarly, if her appearance at a function had to be cancelled at short notice, a rare but not unheard-of event in Finchley, she would never consider a substitute standing in for her. Once, when there was clearly time to arrange for a neighbouring Conservative MP to stand in at an important engagement, she said fiercely: 'No! No! That really isn't necessary and in any case, at this notice they would not be able to come.' It was as clear an instruction as could be given, and the message was obvious: no one substitutes for Margaret Thatcher.

There is in all this a strong lesson for the young, ambitious Tory MP just elected and looking for his first appointment on the Government ladder. My lightly expressed and sympathetic remark after the 1983 landslide victory about the many Conservative back-benchers eyeing so few junior posts in Government brought a small explosion from her. 'Nothing to do! They should be in their constituencies working!' She added, sadly, that she had just discovered that one member of her Cabinet visited his consti-tuency only twice a year.

There is a further incident which illustrates her feelings about Finchley. It happened in 1982 when Downing Street officials were becoming jealous of the amount of time that the Prime Minister spent in Finchley. The longer any Prime Minister is in office, the more jealous Number 10 staff become of anyone or anything that lays claim to its chief occupant. The first warning of just how possessive the civil servants were becoming came from a member of her staff, who said that those at Number 10 were trying to 'steal' part of the Prime Minister's time allocated for Finchley on the grounds that the hours she spent there were 'irrelevant'. Shortly afterwards, Margaret Thatcher herself instructed: 'Don't let them steal constituency time; and if they try and you have any doubts, simply ask them if they have cleared it with me.'

On the day before her next scheduled visit to Finchley I received a phone call from 10 Downing Street. A smooth male voice began by expressing regret that we had not had the pleasure of meeting, which from a civil servant seemed warning enough of what was to come. 'You are expecting the Prime Minister at 4 p.m. tomorrow,' he said. 'I have to tell you that unfortunately you are not going to get her until 5 p.m. Will that be convenient?' My response was: 'Have you cleared this with the Prime Minister?' There was not so much as a pause at the other end of the line before the voice said that he had been just about to do so. He never troubled me again.

Just as Downing Street wanted to save Margaret Thatcher from what it saw as the 'irrelevance' of Finchley, so there was a desire on my part to protect her from some of the constituency's more extreme left-wingers, who to my mind were certainly not members of her Finchley family. She would have none of it. Just as she insisted on none of her time allotted for Finchley being stolen by Downing Street, so she was determined that she should be protected from no one while she was there. She would take on all comers from among the more aggressive of her constituents. On occasions when her constituency surgery was visited by some of Finchley's more belligerent voters, it would accentuate the wonder of the British constitution and its ability to allow one bloody-minded individual constituent to monopolise a large chunk of the time of the British Prime Minister.

The constituency offices themselves were another of the wonders of the British political system, and were a constant source of amazement to the American students who came to Britain as part of their political studies, a few of whom secured the plum posting to the Member of Parliament for Finchley. It would generally take about three months before they understood that they were working for her in her capacity as MP, not as Prime Minister. What none of them could ever get to grips with was the modesty of the premises in which she worked in Finchley, or the demands on her time which constituents could make.

The low level of security upon which she insisted also shocked these Americans. It was plainly obvious that she refused caval-cades of wailing police cars or ostentatiously gun-toting policemen. Though Margaret Thatcher's underwear was not a subject on which I could speak with the remotest authority, it seemed sensible to gently dissuade them from the notion that she wore a bullet-proof vest when she left the converted semi-detached house in Ballards Lane to visit sixty or seventy constituents in another pre-war semi on the other side of Finchley.

Constituents entering the Conservative Association office find the Prime Minister behind her desk with favourite photographs of herself on the walls, including ones taken during the 1979 and 1983 General Election campaigns and another on the day she first reached the Cabinet as Secretary of State for Education. A little over twenty-four hours before her surgery, the Leader of the Opposition and up to 500 other Members of Parliament would have been vying for the precious fifteen minutes on the floor of the Commons when the Prime Minister is available for questioning. In her constituency office, one of the more belligerent of her constituents can be there for up to half an hour. In fact, the rule of the office seems to be that the more belligerent the constituent, the more time is allowed before the Prime Minister says: 'It looks as though we are not going to reach agreement. There is no common ground between us.' It is clearly less of an ordeal for Margaret Thatcher than for outsiders such as the agent, whose instinct when confronted by a rude representative of animal liberationists or militant pensioners, showing total disrespect for the Prime Minister, is to show them the door. Sometimes her eyes will flash; sometimes she will argue and be combative; but never in that Finchley office does she respond to rudeness with rudeness, nor lose her temper.

With those constituents who are simply argumentative or impolite, there is a small tell-tale physical quirk, a sign that she is about to insert the political stiletto and give it a quick turn. With Harold Macmillan it was observed that before he went for the kill in the Commons he would give a little kick with his leg behind the despatch box. With Margaret Thatcher, in the office at 212 Ballards Lane, she will drop her eyes, give a little boxer's jerk of the right shoulder and then hit her opponent verbally as the blue eyes come up flashing. She did it once with dentists who came to the constituency office complaining about pay. She listened quietly to them, then the shoulder jerked and she hit them with the figure showing their average earnings: £26,000 in that year.

This small movement of her shoulder came to be a warning sign for me to wince inwardly in anticipation, as when she launched the Barnet Enterprise Trust in the constituency to foster business development, and a businessman was incautious enough to tell her she could be better occupied than in putting up employers' National Insurance contributions. The shoulder jerked, she snapped that cuts in corporation and other taxes had put £3 billion back into the pockets of business, and she jabbed a finger at the man, demanding: 'So what have you done with it?'

She insists on personally signing letters to constituents, even when almost 8000 were produced by me for new voters in Finchley. Faced with the mountains of letters, she did falter, but only briefly. She remarked wistfully that Mr Reagan – she always called him 'Mr' and never 'President' – had a machine that signed his letters. I put enquiries in hand to discover if such a machine were available in the United Kingdom and whether it could meet the strict security requirements necessary to ensure that no one else would be able to produce perfect copies of her signature. But before the enquiries could result in the production of a machine, she decided: 'I've been signing letters in my constituency for twenty-eight years. If I don't sign these letters, it will demean all those that I have signed in the past.' What the new voters on the electoral register did not realise when the letters landed on their doormats over the coming weeks was that she had signed most of them in the air en route to and from Hong Kong – with a small pile of letters returned afterwards from 10 Downing Street for retyping because the Prime Minister's signature had slipped as her RAF VC10 hit air pockets.

There was one other aspect of her work as MP in Finchley that was initially to flummox me, and that was her ability to remember the names of everyone she met there and the most apparently insignificant aspects of their lives. Thus she would walk of an evening up the front path and into the home of a Conservative

Association member and recall, conversationally, the names of the hostess's children. She would enquire whether the son was still working for a particular oil company, and then remark that the walk to the front door was much nicer now that the path was paved rather than gravelled as it had been the last time she was there, a year or more earlier. Such a phenomenal memory is a boon for any politician and Margaret Thatcher has been putting it to apparently effortless good use in Finchley since the night she was adopted as candidate in 1959. When the Association branches held social functions shortly after her adoption to introduce their new female candidate, then something of a rarity, most charged an entrance fee to recoup their costs. But at one event, the ward chairman decided on holding a raffle instead. Margaret Thatcher said she had an even better idea than a straightforward raffle. She would auction a bottle of scotch – and in doing so she called out the names of everyone in the room to whom she had been introduced just once. She got every name right, and raised £10 for Party funds.

On the eve of the 1983 General Election, she asked me at Chequers when I wanted her 'message' to the Finchley voters – her election address – and promised: 'I will get it to you before I am adopted.' The adoption meeting was a huge media carnival, with television cameras inside the Woodhouse School and 500 members of the Conservative Association packed in with them. Unexpectedly, and for the first time in many years, the entire Thatcher family arrived for the meeting. As the pandemonium died down, Councillor Frank Gibson, the chairman, stood up to move the adoption of Margaret Hilda Thatcher, who was sitting next to me at a table at the head of the hall. At that moment I was aware of something striking my leg under the table. Her memory was faultless as ever, and she was passing over her completed election address. To a professional agent she was a candidate extraordinary.

Even in May 1982, when British troops secured a bridgehead on the Falklands, her memory did not fail her. She was in Finchley that lunch-time and afternoon, but her mind and her heart were on the other side of the Atlantic with the first troops who were going ashore. It had been vital that she went to Finchley as planned so that intelligence signals would not be sent to the Argentinians that something special was happening. That afternoon in Finchley she came across John Mandelberg, director of the Distributive Industries Training Board who had been a contemporary of hers at Oxford thirty years earlier. 'John and I were at college together,' she explained. Then she asked him about his wife. 'How's Felicity?' she enquired.

'I wouldn't have considered keeping on a political career after my marriage had I not been able to arrange it around my family.'

(Margaret Thatcher)

9

DENIS, MARK AND CAROL

OF THE TWO families in Margaret Thatcher's life – the Finchley family and the domestic one – the most remarkable feature is that they simply do not mix. There are few, if any, ties between them despite the thirty years that the two families have run in parallel. The twins Mark and Carol were scarcely off to infants' school when Margaret Thatcher was adopted for and won Finchley for the Conservatives in 1959. It would seem natural to find some key figures in the local Conservative Association who had become close to Mark and Carol over their mother's long involvement with the constituency. Such is the case in many other parliamentary constituencies where the MP is as long-serving as Margaret Thatcher and started out with a young family – leading members of the Association often became unofficial godparents to their local MP's children.

In Finchley, Mark and Carol just do not form a part of their mother's Finchley family. The reason lies in Margaret Thatcher's businesslike approach to everything. She organised her life after her marriage to Denis in 1951 so that it was compartmentalised. With the twins born two years later, she put politics on the back burner and devoted herself to her children. She gave up the Dartford seat which she had fought unsuccessfully in 1950 and

1951, and in the subsequent 1955 General Election stayed on the sidelines. Having spent her first six years of motherhood with the twins – and in studying at home in spare moments for a law degree – she then re-embarked on the road that led to Finchley, Westminster and then the Cabinet table in Downing Street. As she put it herself when she became Leader of the Opposition, she made sure she arranged her career around her family.

In 1959, the year that Margaret Thatcher was selected from 200 applicants as the candidate for Finchley, she and Denis bought 'Dormers', a four-bedroomed detached house in Farnborough, Kent, and installed a nanny named Abbey. The twins were six at the time of the General Election, and it is evidence of the manner in which their mother separates the various elements of her life that they knew nothing of the fever of the hustings until they noticed that the car was covered in rosettes and blue streamers. In the same way, but many years later, Denis and the grown-up twins would be infuriated by a chance remark by Margaret about her appearance in a television programme screened earlier that evening; she had not thought to mention it in time for the family to watch.

She has the rare ability simply to switch off from being politician and become housewife or mother. Before she was elected Opposition Leader it was noticed by her political colleagues that she would rush out of the Finance Bill Committee late at night and change the conversation from the finer points of tax law to her worries about how Carol's studies were going. Even when she was Education Secretary in the 1970–4 Government, she could arrive home at 1 or 2 a.m. but still be up at 6 a.m. to get breakfast for Denis before he left to drive to work in Swindon. Always, then and now, she is anxious to ensure that there is something in the fridge which will provide a quick and nourishing meal. None of this will sound surprising to many working mothers, and she does not regard it as surprising herself, remarking that women are often used to doing many things simultaneously.

The stamina that was required to survive as wife, mother and politician helps to explain her ability to endure in 10 Downing Street in defiance of the predictions that she would burn out or collapse. In fact, she gave warning of this extraordinary stamina shortly after she became Prime Minister, when there was widely expressed surprise at her ability to keep working flat out on as little as four hours' sleep a night. She said: 'Don't forget, I have been going flat out for twenty years. People think that you wake up one fine day and find yourself Prime Minister, having had a laid-back sort of existence. I have never had a laid-back existence. I have always been immensely busy.'

While the school-age twins stayed behind at 'Dormers', looked after by Abbey, their mother travelled first to Finchley to win the seat for the Conservatives, then to Westminster to represent the constituency as Member of Parliament. This compartmentalisation of the domestic family continues in her psychological approach to Finchley to this day. Just as she shrugs off the role of Prime Minister when she crosses the North Circular Road, so she does not take her family with her in her mind. Finchley equals work. Any casual mention of her children while she is there is unlikely to draw a response. When Mark was the focus of public attention over the Cementation affair before he left England to live and work in America, she would arrive in Finchley and very occasionally complain how badly he was being treated by the media. But this was said not as an encouragement to further conversation on the subject, more as a mutter to herself.

The Cementation affair centred around allegations about the reasons why the Sultan of Oman opted for the company Cementation to build a new university. Mark was an adviser to Cementation in one of what seemed to be a succession of less than satisfactory business deals for the son of a Prime Minister. What was important to Margaret Thatcher during the entire affair was that she was being challenged not just as a politician, but as a mother. Inevitably the two roles became intermingled, and Cabinet Ministers who thought they knew her confessed themselves astonished at her protectiveness of Mark. It is not easy being the child of a famous politician. But nor is it easy to be a famous politician and a parent.

Margaret Thatcher ensured, like so many mothers of her

generation, that her children received the benefit of much that she had not enjoyed. The twins had dancing tuition. They had riding lessons. The house was full of toys and fluffy animals (though not real ones, because Denis Thatcher believes that the rightful place for nature is out of doors). Mark is the apple of her eye, and in turn is very proud of his mother and wants to be protective towards her. But he has been overshadowed from birth by two people who are larger in life than most – his mother because of her political success, and his father because not only is he a millionaire businessman but he has a huge, commanding personality. Mark always wanted to be as big as them, but could never quite make it on his own. Even as a child he would pick up the telephone and bark 'Thatcher!' in the manner of his father. But he did not share the judgement of his parents and naively allowed his pursuit of fame and fortune to get him into scrapes that left him even more convinced that the world had a down on him. The storm over his sponsorship by Toyota, the Japanese car manufacturer, in the days when he sought to be a successful racing driver, left him genuinely baffled. He seemed no more to understand the furore when Paul Raymond, the Soho strip-club entrepreneur, stepped in with money to 'rescue' him from the Japanese.

This lack of professional finesse and judgement dogged his business activities until he finally found commercial success, and his wife, in the United States. Even the engagement photograph of Mark and his American bride taken at 10 Downing Street says much about the Prime Minister's son, and caused great wagging of tongues among some members of the Finchley Conservative Association. The reason for this was that virtually the entire group looked so miserable. Mark Thatcher sometimes has that effect on people; he has a heavy spirit and a heavy hand. Like the sons of so many at the top of the political tree, he knows that he can never be as famous or as powerful as his parents, and he seemed, even at his wedding, to be brooding over life's unfairness. He could learn much from his father, Denis, who has lived and worked in the shadow of the first woman Prime Minister in a manner that has enhanced his dignity in the eyes of most people.

In one respect, Mark and his father share the enjoyment of a good party. At a Downing Street reception for the Finchley Conservative Association just after the 1983 General Election, Mark took over the bar at what threatened to be a restrained occasion. The largest proportion of the 182 people thronging Number 10 that evening were pensioners. The balance of gin to tonic poured by Mark ensured rapid conviviality – thanks to him, a jolly good time was had by all.

The pre-wedding reception at Number 10 for Mark and his bride-to-be Diane Burgdorf, as well as the wedding itself, revealed Margaret Thatcher in a guise in which few have seen her: a quiet, retiring, proud but slightly sad mum watching her son with a new Mrs Thatcher. The reception was full of ladies from Dallas with flamboyant dresses, huge false shoulders and mountainously fashioned hair. For a few hours, Number 10 seemed to have become a set for an American soap opera. But for once the bustling, organising hostess that the building knows as Prime Minister was nowhere to be seen; she just faded into the background and let the American noise and colour roll over her. She behaved just as she had when television cameras caught her coming out of St Paul's Cathedral after the wedding of the Prince and Princess of Wales – just another mother at a wedding. After the nuptials of the new Mr and Mrs Thatcher, there was one scene which no one captured on film as the newly-weds set off in their limousine: Margaret and Denis Thatcher standing wordless, holding hands and watching the car disappear out of view.

The difficulty for anyone writing about Mark is to ensure that he rises lightly and happily as a person from the page. He is just not that type of man. But despite his track record for unwittingly embarrassing his mother, he does not lack in filial desire to help and protect her. A rather sad story lies in the manner in which he felt he could best help her before the 1987 General Election. He approached Bernard Ingham, the Number 10 Press Secretary who is closer to Margaret Thatcher than any of her civil servants at 10 Downing Street. What, he asked Ingham, could he do to help his mother during the General Election campaign? Bernard, who shares Margaret Thatcher's ability to get straight to the kernel of a problem, is alleged to have told him: 'Leave the country.' To his credit, Mark did just that.

In Margaret Thatcher's eyes, there is nothing for which Mark requires forgiveness. But if he did, then the absolution of all guilt lies in grandmotherhood. Scarcely have I watched her enthusiasm with children in Finchley without thinking that she will throw herself wholeheartedly into being a grandmother.

Carol Thatcher, too, grew up in the shadow of her mother, and again it showed in the early years that her mother was in Downing Street. As with her twin brother, there was a weariness in her beyond her years as if she accepted, at times with irritation, the loss of individual identity which comes from being a celebrity's child. In her case, she had possibly even more cause than her brother to rue the fact that she was her mother's daughter. The years that Margaret Thatcher was Education Secretary in the 1970–4 Government overlapped with Carol's years reading law at the University of London. Margaret Thatcher was treated badly enough by students, who made her the target of some hatred, but Carol suffered the same bad-mouthing from many of her fellow students through no fault of her own.

Nor is Carol best equipped to deal with the nastier side of life. She is instinctively on the defensive and too ready to think the worst of herself. Once, at a dinner party, the conversation turned to the French language and Carol said she did not speak it at all well. It was a confession that brought from the male guest next to her an offer to teach her. Wine bottles emptied, and Carol insisted that she really did want to improve her inadequate French. By that time the subject was spreading round the table and the room filling with that distinctive sound of the English trying to speak French, but succeeding not very well. What is illustrative of Carol's lack of confidence is that her grasp of French was in fact as good as, if not better than, that of everyone else at the table. But in her self-deprecating manner, she had assumed that everyone else must be better than she is. Over the last two years, however, she has fought her way to independence and a career in journalism in her own right.

Though both twins dote on their mother, there is a sensitivity in Carol's nature that has enabled her to avoid the embarrassments that Mark has brought about with his boundless naivety. For instance, when Carol helped her mother hour by hour through the 1983 General Election campaign, she kept a diary for publication. It was snapped up in advance by Sir David English, editor of the *Daily Mail* and editor-in-chief of the *Mail on Sunday*. Within the newspaper office, a sense of excitement awaited the first pages of the diary that was to tell the inside story of the campaign trail. But as soon as it arrived, the building rang with the sound of executives banging their heads on desks. Carol Thatcher *had* written a diary, but had sensitively neglected to disclose anything that might conceivably embarrass Mum.

Margaret Thatcher was to repay Carol's loyalty with her own in the 1987 General Election. Carol had worked as a writer for Max Hastings, editor of *The Daily Telegraph*, but they had parted under unhappy circumstances. Hastings subsequently made the mistake in the 1987 General Election campaign of joining the party of journalists following the Prime Minister's 'battle bus' which toured the country taking her from one political engagement to another. Though he was a member of the media party, Margaret Thatcher declined to speak to him. By objective standards her decision was wrong but, as in the case of Mark and the Cementation affair, even members of the Opposition are reluctant to criticise her when her family is involved. There is a freemasonry among politicians that crosses party lines when it comes to issues involving their children – they all know how hard it is to be both a good politician and a good parent.

As mother and politician, Margaret Thatcher has set out clearly her views on motherhood and the family. By devoting herself to the twins until they were of school age, then establishing her Finchley family, she behaved in deed much in line with the words she expressed on the subject to the Conservative Women in London in May 1988. It was no new-found philosophy she expressed, but it represents so much of what she has always believed about women and their families.

[119]

We support the right of women to choose our own lives for ourselves. If women wish to be lawyers, doctors, engineers, scientists, we should have the same opportunities as men. More and more we do. In the last ten years, the number of women becoming solicitors has doubled. The number of doctors graduating is up by over 50 per cent and the number of women becoming chartered accountants has increased threefold.

But many women wish to devote themselves mainly to raising a family and running a home. And we should have that choice too. Very few jobs can compare in long-term importance and satisfaction with that of house-wife and mother. For the family is the building block of society. It is a nursery, a school, a hospital, a leisure centre, a place of refuge and a place of rest. It encompasses the whole of society. It fashions our beliefs. It is the preparation for the rest of our life. And women run it.

The State must look after some children in care and those old people who cannot look after themselves. But the family is responsible for an infinitely greater number of children and far more elderly people. However much welfare the State provides, the family provides more – much more.

Reflecting on the consequences of the collapse of parental example and guidance, she told Conservatives in Harrogate in March 1982:

We are reaping what was sown in the sixties. The fashionable theories and permissive claptrap set the scene for a society in which the old virtues of discipline and self-restraint were denigrated.

Parents, teachers and other adults need to set clear, consistent limits to the behaviour of children and young people. Children need, respond to, and too often lack, clear rules consistently, firmly, fairly and effectively applied. Only in this way will they be able to grow up in a framework of certainty and learn the self-control necessary to cope with the problems of life.

Children learn by example, and the most powerful influence on their life is what they learn at home and at school.

When she talks politically about the family, she has her own home life very much in mind.

Denis Thatcher has behaved in public as if he were consort to a queen. He has scrupulously avoided publicity, shunned inter-views, often walked three paces behind her at official functions as if taking lessons from the Duke of Edinburgh, and conveyed the general impression to the world that he keeps a certain distance from Margaret Thatcher as Prime Minister. The reality is very different.

Margaret Thatcher launched into her Party Conference speech in Brighton a little over a year after her first General Election victory in 1979 by referring to the fact that her Cabinet colleagues all have junior Ministers. She went on: 'At Number 10, I have no junior Ministers. There is just Denis and me – and I could not do without him.' To suggest that Denis is an *ex officio* member of the Government or a special adviser to the Prime Minister is to misunderstand what politics are about. But there is not the slightest doubt that he is a major influence on her. It is impossible for a man of such strong views and who is as respected by her as he is not to colour her environment and thinking.

Margaret Roberts and Denis Thatcher were married in the Wesleyan Chapel in London on 13 December 1951, and neither of them could have guessed as they took their marriage vows that the bride was to become Prime Minister of Great Britain and Northern Ireland and that the bridegroom would be in a position to wake up in Number 10 in May 1979 to offer his advice on how the country should be run. However, any guest at the wedding must have known that the bride was an extraordinary woman. Her dress was not white but sapphire blue and, extraordinarily, it was a replica of one worn by Georgiana, Duchess of Devonshire, in a painting by Gainsborough. It was matched by a sapphire hat with ostrich feathers.

Denis Thatcher had been divorced a year before he met Margaret Roberts while she was fighting to win Dartford for the Conservatives in 1950 and again in 1951. In fact, they met on the night of her adoption as candidate in Dartford. Ten years older than her, he was already financially well off. He was managing director of the family paint and wallpaper company, a Methodist like her, drove a Jaguar car and lived in Chelsea. Educated at Mill Hill public school, he had served with the Royal Artillery in France, Sicily and Italy and had been mentioned in despatches. He is reported to have been then what he certainly is today – a man of strongly held

[121]

opinions, most of them of an ultra-Conservative nature. When his wife went on, twenty-eight years after they had married, to become Prime Minister, he saw that as no reason for him to stop expressing those opinions. Indeed, how could he stop the habit of a lifetime?

Over the years since Margaret and Denis Thatcher moved into the flat over 10 Downing Street, the policies of the Government have come more into line with his own views. He has held much the same opinions since long before his wife became Prime Minister. At cocktail parties in the months after the 1979 General Election, Denis Thatcher could be heard expressing his views on issues such as unemployment, and they sounded positively reactionary. Why, he would ask Tory MPs, could firms he was associated with not fill vacancies when unemployment was a so-called political problem? In those days it seemed to be a question that was almost indecent in polite company, certainly to the ears of some of the less robust Conservative back-benchers. Since then, the Government's attention to publicising the opportunities for training and re-training, and the wide acceptance that some of the 'unemployed' in the South are as yet untraced swindlers of State benefits, have made it more reasonable for Denis Thatcher's question to be asked in political circles.

Denis is often caricatured as something of a blimpish half-wit who spends his time playing golf and drinking large gin and tonics. In London's West End the comedy 'Anyone for Denis?' was based on this caricature, and both he and Margaret Thatcher sat through it – to raise a substantial sum of money for charity. But the caricature is just that – a caricature. He is a shrewd businessman who has run his own firm and then gone on to sit on major company boards. At one Downing Street reception party he was describing just how inaccurate was the caricature of himself – until he spoiled it when a golfing friend approached to remark on a wonderful day on the golfing links. Denis cried 'Brilliant shot, wasn't it?' then used his gin and tonic to imitate the action of a three iron. The true explanation is that the keen financial mind and strong political views complement a personality that is larger than life. This all combines to make a man who is immensely good fun.

The influence of Denis on the Prime Minister stems from the sheer consistency of his views. He is a rock. She is a politician who leans on him. He expresses his views to her in what her civil servants call 'unsupervised time'. In the view of the Civil Service, Ministers cannot be trusted totally unless supervised. However, even the highest echelons of the Civil Service have yet to devise a way of keeping an eye on the Prime Minister when she goes to bed, gets up and eats her breakfast.

Over the years since 1979, some of the details of this 'unsupervised time' have emerged. For example, Margaret Thatcher listens to BBC Radio's *Today* programme, which explains why so many ambitious junior Ministers would stay up all night for a three-minute slot on it in the hope that she might be impressed by their performance. Denis watches breakfast television, and husband and wife exchange shouted comments about the day's news.

Just what effect the views of Denis and the twins have on Margaret Thatcher, and thus on the governance of Britain, is locked in the mind of the Prime Minister. The degree of influence could perhaps be judged from one remark she made when she was asked by children in her constituency about the need to take into account advice from children. She replied that she does not take *advice* from her family, but that it was useful to hear their views.

What is the personal relationship between Margaret and Denis Thatcher? The image of Denis walking three paces behind his wife is deceptive. In fact, if he issues a command, she will take her lead from him without question. In the 1983 General Election campaign, when she was running behind her timetable her organisers would manipulate Denis to persuade her to get a move on. 'Come on Margaret' he would shout, and she would fall in line without a murmur. Similarly, during the 1987 campaign when both were in Reading in Berkshire, she visited a factory and the trip went as smoothly as Conservative Central Office had planned until the factory owner next door buttonholed the Prime Minister. He insisted that she should visit his factory as well, and the Prime Minister strode off behind him until the voice of Denis rang out:

'No you don't, Margaret! You haven't got time!' Without hesitation she performed a perfect U-turn and was back in line. In public she will not gainsay him. In turn, his role in the public arena is to act with a combination of dignity suitable to the occasion and pride in his wife.

Away from the public eye, the relationship can sometimes be different. For instance, in March 1984 at the Barnet Mayor's Ball, by the time the Prime Minister arrived I had received a warning in advance from 10 Downing Street that she was tired and did not really want to attend because the day had been long and exhausting. Accordingly, at 11 p.m. I suggested to her that it was time to leave. 'No! No!' she said, and went back to signing programmes as souvenirs for the guests who were queueing up at her table. More time passed, and one of her Special Branch officers sidled up and whispered to me that Denis Thatcher wanted to leave. Again, I suggested to her that the moment for departure had arrived. 'No,' she said, 'I'm enjoying myself.' Next, Denis Thatcher himself was at my elbow. His request was simple: 'I want to go. Get the woman out of here.' (He does not always describe the Prime Minister as his wife.) After two rebuffs from the Prime Minister, a better idea came to mind. 'You do it, Mr Thatcher,' I said. He pulled himself up, said 'Right!' and strode to where she was sitting at the table talking. He stood over her and said in something more than a murmur 'Come along, darling.' With hardly so much as a glance at him, she put out her hand, took his arm and gently pulled him down into a vacant chair at the table. He sat there for fifteen minutes, her hand resting firmly on his arm, before she rose, he followed and they left.

On the major domestic decisions he wears the trousers and she bows to his judgement. After a week at Westminster and Downing Street she might want to head for Chequers and the peace of the Buckinghamshire countryside late on a Friday night after she has finished in Finchley. Instead, she will head for the flat above her Downing Street office until Denis returns from an evening with friends or business acquaintances – because that is what he wants. Watching them together is like seeing any couple who have learned over nearly forty years to live with the excesses and foibles of the other. Denis is partial to drink and colourful language, both of which Margaret clearly gave up trying to moderate many years ago, although they are not tolerated by her without the occasional reproachful cluck, or eyes raised to the ceiling in female disapproval.

By preference Margaret would probably have looked for a retirement home in or around Oxford, rather than Dulwich in central London. The Dulwich home was Denis's choice. Similarly, she would probably give up politics and power for him if he were adamant about it. Half-way through the 1983–7 Parliament, when some Conservatives at Westminster were looking to see whether Margaret Thatcher would stand down, the word that passed between them was: 'Denis is the key.'

In fact Denis has at least once suggested that his wife chuck it all in – back in the dark days when she was Education Secretary in Edward Heath's Government. They were years when she was bruised not just politically but physically, too, by the sheer violence that was stirred up by the Labour Party and students against the 'Milk Snatcher' who had ended free school milk. Isolated in the Cabinet, she became a hate figure in the media and the Commons where, whenever she appeared, Labour MPs would chant 'Ditch the bitch'. Finally, at an angry demonstration by polytechnic students in Liverpool, an egg was thrown at her: not a chicken's egg, but a stone egg. It hit her on the chest, bruising her badly. The injury was not realised until later because, though she admitted that it 'hurt like mad', she had continued with her speech. Denis urged her to throw in the towel, but she declined. In those early years, she would often say: 'They are not going to break me.'

Two stories illustrate the depth of their relationship. The first, in 1983 when they were on holiday together in Switzerland, saw the couple walking up the lower slopes of a mountain, leaving their Special Branch officer sitting watchfully at the lakeside. They returned and sat by a jetty, saying nothing and looking at the lake until Denis said: 'Come on Thatcher. I feel a gin and tonic coming on.' She immediately stood up and followed him. There is no doubt among those who have watched the couple as to the fact that

Denis is the key to her future in Number 10. For if one day Denis says 'That's it Thatcher – time for retirement' then she will follow, wherever retirement may be.

The second incident occurred just before the 1983 General Election when she called me to Chequers on 14 May to help prepare for the campaign in Finchley. Carol had just arrived unexpectedly from Australia and so the preparations for the General Election were interrupted by a five-course meal and celebrations that put the programme well behind schedule.

It was past 10 p.m. before Margaret got down to discussing details of the campaign, and at around 1 a.m. she set off to look for her typewriter to finish writing her election address, a document to which she attaches great importance because it goes through the letterbox of every door in Finchley. Denis had fallen asleep in a chair and awoke as she disappeared from the room in search of the machine. 'Where is the woman?' he demanded. She hurried back and began an explanation. Immediately, he ordered me to go home. To her, he snorted: 'What are you doing?' Seeing the typewriter and notes for writing the election address, he added: 'Is this your election address you are going to write? Surely you don't think people are going to read the thing, do you woman?' If Denis was bad-tempered, it was not with the 'woman' or 'Thatcher' but with the whole paraphernalia of elections and power which keeps his wife up to the early hours. He was being – and not for the first time in my presence – protective of the private person. He wanted me out of the building; it was bedtime. He believes that everyone – her agent, the Cabinet, Downing Street staff, the Conservative Party and the nation at large – makes too many demands on his wife. He is immensely proud of her and wants only to protect her, albeit in his somewhat Edwardian manner.

Despite the pressures of politics and their inevitable intrusion into family life, Margaret and Denis Thatcher and Carol and Mark have secured one fundamental achievement as a family; even today they remain just that – a family. Despite all the demands on them, their get-togethers and reunions are more frequent than in many other 'ordinary' families.

[126]

'She's both a role model and an anti-role model; she's such a strong woman and so striking that people react violently either for or against her.' (Mary Archer)

10

WILFUL POLITICIAN

MARGARET THATCHER has probably been the object of more personal abuse than any other Prime Minister this century. It is not just that she has been in office so long. She produces extreme reactions in people regardless of the length of time the public has had to become accustomed to her as Prime Minister. Some of the recorded remarks do not simply drip with venom but appear to have been carefully marinated in it. Jonathan Miller, when asked why the vast majority of the intellectual and cultural establishment are so deeply hostile to her, responded: 'Isn't the reason self-evident? It's the same as why the bulk of the human race is hostile to typhoid.' Miller went on to say that he found her 'loathsome, repulsive in almost every way'.

It is in the art world and among intellectuals that the hatred of Margaret Thatcher seems to be deepest. It is perhaps significant that the art world had become increasingly dependent on the patronage of the State, to which Margaret Thatcher is so opposed, for their financing. In addition, academics have perhaps double reason to dislike her. Not only had they grown to believe under the years of socialism that theirs was a right to State support almost regardless of their contribution to the nation, but Thatcherism turned upside down most of the intellectual and social arguments they had developed since the Second World War.

The attitudes of Britain's cultural and intellectual elite were chronicled in the *Daily Express* in a brilliantly researched article by Graham Turner which also illuminated other reasons for the antipathy. Baroness Warnock, Mistress of Girton College, Cambridge, said the rational explanation for why academics hate her so much is her total lack of understanding of what universities are about. Margaret Thatcher wouldn't lose a wink of sleep, except politically, she said, if Oxford and Cambridge were sold off to ICI, so long as the price was right. Then, perhaps getting nearer to a genuine reason for what she conceded was a detestation among most academics for Margaret Thatcher, Baroness Warnock said that there were also deep personal objections to her. The way she shouted people out was the worst of the lower middle classes, she continued. Her patronising, elocutionary voice was like a primary school headmistress losing patience with the children. And she also cited the neat, well-groomed clothes and hair 'packaged together in a way that's not exactly vulgar, just low'. Odious suburban gentility just about summed up that side of Margaret Thatcher, said the Mistress of Girton. She felt 'a kind of rage' whenever she thought about her.

All of this raises a number of questions. What is wrong with the lower middle classes? What's wrong with primary school headmistresses? And what is wrong with being neat, well groomed and having hair that is 'packaged' instead of unkempt, which is the way some academic women seem to wear it? The plain fact is that the Mistress of Girton identified precisely why not only the ladies of the Conservative Associations love Margaret Thatcher and always have, but, as three General Elections have shown, why so many women who do not belong to the Conservative Party will vote for her and what she stands for.

It is a matter of immense satisfaction to Margaret Thatcher that the lower middle classes are expanding rapidly under her Government, but it is no good pretending that she does not care what is said about her. At the personal level the abusive criticism hurts. She has conceded publicly that she is often accused of 'lecturing or preaching', but rationalised it to her Party Conference audience this way:

> I suppose it is a critic's way of saying 'Well, we know it is true but we have to carp at something.' I do not care about that. But I do care about the future of free enterprise, the jobs and exports it provides and the independence it brings out in people.

Similarly, she said on a later occasion: 'I do not greatly care what people say about me. I do greatly care what people think about our country.'

Significantly, her statement to the Conservative faithful was crafted to give the impression of not caring what people say about her, although it in fact conceded that she does care a bit. Once, in an early interview in a women's magazine, she let slip that she cries sometimes at night when everything seems to be too much for her. In a subsequent Commons debate, her remark had Labour's Dennis Skinner, known with great accuracy as the 'Beast of Bolsover, snarling that he would like to see her cry.

She has learned a lesson since then and decided, quite consciously, that she will not expose herself to sources of unnecessary pain. She was once asked, for instance, if she watched the satirical television programme *Spitting Image*, in which a cruelly lifelike puppet of herself can be seen, waistcoated and smoking a cigar, leaving the gents' toilet buttoning its fly. 'Why should I watch it?' she responded. 'They only want to hurt me.' So in addition to the broad back which is every politician's prerequisite before going anywhere near the hustings, she has built a second protective shield around herself. From behind the shield there operates a strong will.

Among her officials in Number 10 she has merely to cough for them to drop a line of argument and begin on another. When in the presence of officials from Conservative Central Office she has on occasion been heard wondering aloud, as she did once at a meeting at Number 10 about an official who was being difficult, 'Should we withdraw our love?' Such is the deceptively gentle expression that she can use at times in determining someone's future.

In Finchley she employs a repertoire ranging from similar gentle understatements to simply changing the agenda to get her way. She can also achieve her aim with the infuriating knack of apparently refusing to understand what she is being told, as in 1983 when figures were published showing how many council homes had been sold nationally under her Government's new right-to-buy law. At face value the statistics for sales of council houses in Barnet in her constituency did not look at all good: only 300 council homes had been sold since the law was passed. The figures were too promising an opportunity for the Labour Party at Westminster to miss, and soon they were claiming that the Prime Minister did not have the support of her own local council or local people for the right-to-buy law, one of her most prized pieces of legislation. She was stung by the allegations and phoned Councillor Leslie Pym, leader of the Conservatives on Barnet Council, from her office at the Commons. The next time she visited the Finchley Conservative Association office, he was there to explain himself and his council. What he pointed out, with some justification, was that to its credit the council was running way ahead of the new laws and had notched up no less than 1700 sales of council homes even before the right-to-buy law had been passed by Parliament. It seemed that Councillor Pym had a good argument, but every time he told her she was forgetting all the homes sold before the law was passed, she replied that *he* was forgetting that her Government had recently passed a right-to-buy law. She simply refused to understand that homes had been sold voluntarily by the council before the law gave tenants a statutory right to buy.

At the end of the meeting both the Prime Minister and Councillor Pym refused to accept each other's argument, but the message to him was plain enough: accelerate council home sales. Three years later total sales had reached 4000. Later, at a crowded function attended by, among others, Councillor Pym, she said to him: 'Four thousand homes sold: Really? That many? Why, that's marvellous. Now tell me, how did that happen?' Until then I had been prepared to believe that she might be just a simple politician. But this was the first occasion on which I had positive proof that she really is a very astute lady who thinks, plans and remembers over a very long time scale.

She has an immensely strong will, although she can be hurt and wounded and even falter in her beliefs, as when she had wondered aloud, while signing Christmas cards during the miners' strike, whether she was right to be continuing with the dispute. But what is invariably dominant within her is that extremely strong will. Whether this wilfulness comes from her being a woman is an unanswerable question. She is the only woman Prime Minister Britain has ever had, so there can be no comparisons. However, it is clear that John Nott, her Defence Secretary during the Falklands crisis, believes that her strength of will stems from her femininity. He said that no man would have taken the Task Force to the point of forcing the Argentinians to surrender; a man would have compromised, he said.

She has always been an assiduous Member of Parliament for Finchley when dealing with constituency issues. On occasions being Prime Minister helps – civil servants and Ministers would be less than human if they did not take special care when a letter from Mrs Thatcher reaches their desk. But under the United Kingdom system of government, even Prime Ministers who have been in 10 Downing Street as long as Margaret Thatcher have to fight their way through the Whitehall machine on behalf of their constituents like any other of the 650 MPs. Margaret Thatcher is just that – MP not PM. She would not want it any other way.

In Finchley Margaret Thatcher would sometimes exercise her will with the blunt force of a sledgehammer. At one stage a public enquiry was being held to decide on a recommendation as to whether or not to widen a road crossing East Finchley. Councillor Pym complained to her that the Labour Party was scoring successes over the Ministry of Transport team. Within days, an almost entirely new team of high-fliers was fielded by the Ministry of Transport. Margaret Thatcher had called Lynda Chalker, then Junior Transport Minister, to one side at Westminster and told her: 'Sort it!'

On other occasions she would use her power with great gentleness, as in the case of St Mary's School which, when I arrived as agent, was struggling to avoid becoming a slum. It was clear that she should visit the school as a priority. When she arrived, the headmistress joked with underlying seriousness that the walls were being held up by the sticking paper on the children's paintings. The Prime Minister revealed that ten years earlier when she was Secretary of State for Education in Edward Heath's Government, she had ordered the replacement of the St Mary's structure and had put it in the Department's 'pool' for rebuilding. As soon as she had left the Department with the advent of the Labour Government, St Mary's had been taken out of the pool.

She arranged for a delegation to visit Sir Keith Joseph, Secretary of State at the Department of Education. Sir Keith is by nature a thinker rather than an administrator. He was also the philosophical architect of much of what is now called Thatcherism. It may have been because of the special place he holds in her affections that when his Department did not give St Mary's the answer the Prime Minister expected, he received a mild letter from her suggesting that he had been given 'bad advice' by his officials. A second meeting with Sir Keith was arranged, fresh advice was issued, and the rebuilding of St Mary's was subsequently approved.

The gentleness with which Sir Keith was treated over his gaffe and the embarrassment it caused for the Prime Minister may also have been due in part to the personal experience she had had of officials at the Department of Education. Many of them had made her very angry and dissatisfied during her time as Secretary of State for Education. They believed that they had a special insight into what children needed from the education system, a view that she felt to be totally divorced from the wishes of parents and the demands of working life.

In securing her objectives, whether in Finchley or in Government, she is always armed with facts and figures. When Harold (now Lord) Wilson was Prime Minister he made a virtue in public of his phenomenal memory. I suspect that hers is equally remarkable, but she does not boast about it; she simply uses it. Her debut in the Commons as a Minister is still remembered by some of the old political hands as a demonstration of well-researched and well-remembered facts. She had been appointed Joint Parliamentary Secretary to the Ministry of Pensions and National Insurance, and reeled off statistics like sparks from a catherine wheel. She whirled off the relative values of pensions in 1946, 1951, 1959 and 1962, the cost of living in smoking and non-smoking households, the total spent on pensions, the total raised in surtax, and the levels of pensions in Sweden, Denmark and West Germany. For forty-two minutes she hardly stopped to draw breath – and it was by no means an isolated display.

Earlier, on her appointment to the Opposition front bench, she had stunned the Commons and drawn gasps when she mentioned in an aside that she had read every Budget speech and every Finance Bill since 1946. It was research that paid off, because she used it so effectively against the Labour Government that Iain Macleod, a Conservative intellectual giant of his day, described her speech as the first triumph by a woman he had ever heard in the Commons. Sadly for Great Britain, he did not live to see that woman flower into leader and stateswoman.

Her appetite for statistics was to prove insatiable. When she was appointed to the Shadow Cabinet and was used by Edward Heath to wind up for the Conservative Opposition in a debate on the Labour Government's prices policy, she arrived at the despatch box with such a well-researched case that she was able to destroy the myth that the outgoing Conservative Government had left an £800-million deficit. Later, the *Daily Telegraph* wondered aloud why, when the Commons library was open to 240 Conservative MPs, only one – Margaret Thatcher – had gone there to do her homework.

It is difficult to exaggerate either the extent to which research underpins her authority and power or the liking she has for statistics of any sort. Knowledge is power, and she loves retaining almost any sort of knowledge, although with something more than the lawyer's ability to read rapidly and retain facts for only as long as is necessary for a case.

In Finchley it became necessary, before she went to meet any company officials, for me to warn the executives that they should be armed with more than the facts and figures relevant to the case in hand. She had to be second-guessed on the most far-flung questions that might come to mind. So when McDonalds, the hamburger chain which has its headquarters in Finchley, ran into problems with the European Community, I gave its executives the appropriate warning: it would be no good just being able to explain their own specific problem (which involved McDonalds being unable to take their hamburgers across national frontiers). When the meeting took place it developed, as I had suspected it would, into an exploration by Margaret Thatcher of the life of a hamburger. First she wanted to know the total number of stores that the company had world-wide. Then she wanted to know the total number of hamburgers produced by the company each year. Along the way, she needed to know how many head of cattle were required for slaughtering each year to make the hamburgers. The likelihood is that she could still recite those hamburger statistics today.

It is this enquiring and researching mind, coupled with such a retentive memory and the ability to get to the very heart of the most complex of issues, which underpin her will and authority. She has only to see the brief of a fellow Minister to absorb and understand it possibly better than he or she has. Her knowledge can be displayed in a startling manner and at the most unexpected moments. Over the dinner table she will pick up a conversational point and, for example, use it to launch into a detailed argument about the United States, using as her ammunition the precise percentage breakdown, to the second decimal point, of its current population into those of Irish, Italian or German extraction. With equal ease, she will discuss the relative merits of ancient and modern Japanese pearl culture, backed by a battery of facts and figures, all based on one short visit to a Japanese pearl specialist during her first visit to the Far East as Prime Minister.

Only once did I see her memory fail, and that was when she flew to India on a hastily arranged visit for the funeral of the assassinated Indian Prime Minister Indira Gandhi. She had been given a cheque for charity and in the rush for the plane simply forgot to do anything with it except stuff it in her handbag. When she saw representatives of the charity some weeks later she said that the cheque had gone with her to India for security reasons. 'My staff in Number 10 know that the safest place for any document is in my handbag,' she explained.

Her strong-willed determination is evidenced in the heart of suburban Finchley by a small area of rural conservation the existence of which is due entirely to her intervention. The area is part of an old Electricity Board building and site which fell into disrepair and was eventually redeveloped by a businessman as a headquarters for his companies. Margaret Thatcher agreed to open the new building and used the occasion as an opportunity to tell the businessman, Stephen Rubin, that the surrounding 4.5 acres could be usefully landscaped and conserved as an area of natural beauty. Some months later she returned to the company headquarters for the launch of the Barnet Enterprise Trust, a scheme designed to encourage new small businesses. She looked at the surrounding and still largely derelict area and repeated, still as charmingly to Stephen Rubin as on the first occasion although somewhat more bluntly: 'This area could be usefully turned into an area of natural beauty.' He got the message. She returned to the building for a third time in July 1987 to see her proposal turned into the reality of a lake restocked with fish and surrounded by new trees and bushes.

Faced with a wilful woman armed with facts and figures, the intelligent question is how best to disarm her. Confronting her is easy; anyone can do that, and lose. Winning against her is the hard part. The best way is to approach her with an argument that is presented crisply and knowledgeably, then stick with it as she tries to find the weak spots. She is intolerant of intellectual slackness, of threadbare arguments and of poor advocacy. She enjoys a good, businesslike argument, provided it is based on solid facts. She always demands thorough research to back up cases, both her own and those of others; this is one of her strongest weapons in advancing her beliefs and objectives. The incautious Minister who fails to learn his Whitehall brief thoroughly will soon find that she has absorbed it in greater detail than he has – and that now she is using it against him. Politics and Government are a very serious, professional business for her. It may seem today that these have always been serious and professional matters, but in earlier days it was too often necessary in the Conservative Party to be a gifted amateur, *bon viveur* and wit as a prerequisite to advancement. Margaret Thatcher, however, prefers a good argument to a good joke.

Two examples illustrate her approach. The first concerns one of her bright back-benchers with entrepreneurial flair – his own thriving company as proof of it – and a political philosophy that was certainly in tune with her own. The first step on the ladder of Government seemed to beckon him. He was confident on the floor of the Commons, and held the promise of being a good administrator. It is known that Margaret Thatcher thought well of him and the Government Chief Whip had no black mark against him. But at a drinks party at Number 10, the back-bencher made a flippant aside about the need for a Government post so that the Royal Air Force could give him a lift to his far-flung constituency. The crashing of his promotion prospects was written in the Prime Minister's face. She does not understand many jokes, and certainly not those from ambitious MPs who want to be among her Ministers. The black mark was dutifully noted by the Government Chief Whip.

The second incident involves John Major when he was a Government Whip with special responsibilities for liaising between the Treasury and back-bench MPs. He was a last-minute invitee to a Downing Street dinner, the invitation having been engineered by the Government Chief Whip. Major was seated two chairs away from the Prime Minister at the dining table, and she asked him about a particular clause in the Finance Bill and how it should be handled in the Standing Committee of MPs considering it. She clearly wanted to have something more than a sociable chat, and it transpired that she disagreed with Major about the handling of the clause. The discussion became more and more detailed, and to John Major's embarrassment it was taking place over and around the guest seated between him and the Prime Minister. Margaret is no slouch when it comes to knowing the details of a post-war Finance Bill, but John Major stuck to his guns. At the end of the evening as he left Number 10, Denis Thatcher, who had also been at the table, patted him warmly on the back and said 'Well done.' John Major took this to be a consoling gesture from Denis, and set off morosely to the telephone to tell his wife that his political career was over. It was hopeless, he said – he had been invited to 10 Downing Street to dinner by the Prime Minister and had spent most of it arguing with her.

Shortly afterwards, he was promoted to his first ministerial post and shot rapidly into the Cabinet as Chief Secretary to the Treasury. He had guessed that evening when he was invited to Downing Street that the Chief Whip was arranging for him to go on trial. What he had not realised was that he would have failed had he tried to be merely sociable, humorous or pliant. The serious conviction with which she holds her beliefs, expresses them and then challenges others to argue her out of them is one of the most striking features of Margaret Thatcher's character to anyone dealing with her in politics. Cabinet Ministers and civil servants alike have noted from the start of her years in Number 10 how she comes out of her corner fighting her case, and expects others to do the same. There is no cautious manoeuvring, no stealthy stalking, but rather a straightforward exposition of where she stands. She has even taken her forthrightness into the Cabinet, where the traditional role of the Prime Minister is that of chairman rather than the first advocate to speak. When Douglas Hurd, now the Home Secretary, first went on to senior Cabinet committees and then the Cabinet itself, he expressed surprise to close friends at her style. Leading as she did from the hip and the lip left her exposed if the rest of the meeting took a somewhat different position to hers and she was forced to backtrack. Having put forward her position, she could act only with difficulty in the role of chairman summing up the meeting. What happened in practice was that it would often be left to Viscount Whitelaw, her deputy, to sum up at the conclusion.

Some Cabinet Ministers – and more particularly ex-Cabinet ministers – have argued that it is difficult to deal with such a wilful Prime Minister when the holder of the post is a woman. They feel inhibited by her femininity. How on earth, they have asked, can you speak openly and forcefully with a woman using the same strong language as you would with a man? The old public-school Conservative often simply does not understand the female of the species. They fail to appreciate that this Prime Minister needs to be treated as a woman and not – and this is the crucial difference – with the apologetic approach of someone who wishes she were a man.

The success of Cecil Parkinson is in some measure due to his ability to appreciate and understand that she is a woman as well as Prime Minister. There is one example that bears it out perfectly. On the Saturday, 14 May 1983, before she called her first General Election as Prime Minister and named 9 June as the day, Margaret Thatcher called me to Chequers to discuss arrangements for her campaign in Finchley. The date of the election was not yet known and she did not divulge it to me because, as subsequent events showed, she had not decided upon it. Once more, the woman who is usually so decisive and wilful was uncertain and hesitant. This was the first time she had called a General Election. If she got the timing of it wrong, and thus achieved the wrong result, then by her own hand she would be throwing away her power. The choice was between 9 and 23 June, and as the outcome was a Conservative majority of 144, the decision seems irrelevant with the benefit of hindsight. But it certainly did not feel that way to her at the time. On the Sunday, Cecil Parkinson, then Party Chairman, arrived with a posse of other Cabinet Ministers. It was his task to make a presentation of the campaign plans and then lead into a discussion of the date. He wanted 9 June. She did not know what to do, and the choice seemed so wide open that the next day Robin Oakley in the *Daily Mail* covered the front page with the wrong date and claimed that the election would be held on 23 June.

Though Cecil Parkinson was determined that the election should be on 9 June, he realised that his chances of securing this date would be strong only as long as he did not press, cajole or question. His tactics that afternoon had been to set out his presentation, to discuss and to argue his case, but not to press, demand of her or put requests to her. Late that night he allowed the conversation simply to die away, and watched as the Prime Minister fell silent and stared long into the embers of the fire. He knew that she was finally settling on 9 June when she said: 'But the Queen might not be able to see me tomorrow in any event, even if I wanted to see her.' Such an audience with the Queen would have been necessary that Monday if the monarch were to dissolve Parliament for a 9 June General Election.

It was then that Ian Gow, her Parliamentary Private Secretary, jumped to his feet and scurried from the room, saying: 'I'll phone the Palace and find out.' He returned to say that the Queen could indeed see the Prime Minister next morning should she wish to discuss the dissolution of Parliament and the calling of a General Election. Cecil Parkinson knew that he had got the date he wanted, but he was shrewd enough to say nothing more on the subject. He simply went home. The next morning the Prime Minister went to Buckingham Palace and the General Election was called for 9 June.

'A woman's work is never done.'

(Margaret Thatcher)

11

HER POLITICAL VISION

WHAT IS THE ultimate aim of Margaret Thatcher – her vision for the British people? Clearly she wants Britain great again, and its record of economic growth under her Premiership is unequalled in post-war history. But there is more to the greatness of a nation than its industry and national finances. For Margaret Thatcher, the people will be great again when the majority of them want to plant trees. For her, trees have immense symbolism. As she told the Conservative Party Conference in Brighton in 1982: 'In the fifties and sixties the fashion was to say that the long term does not matter very much because, as Maynard Keynes put it, "In the long run we are all dead." Anyone who thought like that would never plant a tree.'

Even after nearly nine years of Thatcherism, in October 1987 when the greatest hurricane for two centuries destroyed millions of trees in southern England, some of her closest Ministers failed to recognise the importance of trees, both symbolic and practical, to her. In the immediate aftermath of the hurricane, a meeting of Cabinet and other Ministers was called under the chairmanship of Douglas Hurd, the Home Secretary, with Nicholas Ridley, the Environment Secretary, among its members. Towards the end of the meeting Ridley suggested that a Government-financed tree-planting programme should be put in hand. The proposal was laughed out by the committee, most of whom were concerned entirely with the short-term problems of transport dislocation caused by the hurricane. Ridley – who is one of the few Cabinet Ministers who can demand and get instant access to Margaret Thatcher without even having to specify the reason – took his demand to Number 10. He did so in the belief that while guffaws were ringing round Whitehall, she would agree with him. She did, and the Government moved immediately to address the problem of the gaping wounds in the forests and city centres. What Ridley understood instinctively, as did she, is that trees represent strength, growth, stability and continuity through the ages.

The association between the new Conservative Party of Margaret Thatcher and the landed, aristocratic gentry is perhaps weaker now than it has ever been, but if there is a link between the meritocracy of today and the inherited wealth of yesterday, then it is represented by her relationship with Nicholas Ridley. As members of an old, land-owning family, Ridley's forefathers would plant saplings that they knew would grow into majestic trees when they were long dead. They planted with an eye to a tomorrow they would never see. Though Margaret Thatcher is accused of creating a selfish, 'short-termist' society, her views about the planting of trees symbolise the long-term side to the society she wants to create. She believes that if people are given the opportunity to create wealth, they will use it in ways that will ensure they are remembered long after they are dead: the construction of magnificent buildings, bestowing endowments, making philanthropic gestures – and creating broad-leaved forests.

Margaret Thatcher believes that one of the tenets of Conservatism is that the more successful you are, the greater your obligations and responsibilities to family, community and country, and it follows that part of her vision for the future is to recapture some of the spirit of the past. She is fond of saying, as she has to me, that if you look back you will find that our great cities were built by the city fathers. They created employment and wealth, but they did not stop there. They went on to build schools, hospitals, libraries and art galleries. Far from the selfish society which her critics claim she is intent on, her aim is for a *less* selfish one. Just as the British people responded to incentives to work when she provided them with an incentive society, so she believes that they will respond with acts of charity and generosity as new wealth is accumulated. She said in Brighton in 1988, 'I want the generous society.'

Her vision is summed up by one comment she made.

We are in the business of planting trees for our children and grandchildren, or we have no business to be in politics at all. We are not a one-generation party. We do not intend to let Britain become a one-generation society.

Later in the same speech she was to move the environment issue to the centre of the political stage with this quote.

We Conservatives are not merely Friends of the Earth – we are its guardians and trustees for generations to come. The core of Tory philosophy and the case for protecting the environment are the same.

No generation has a freehold on this earth, all we have is a life tenancy – with a full repairing lease – and this Government intends to meet the terms of that lease in full.

It has been said that you can tell a woman by what she keeps in her handbag, and in the case of Margaret Thatcher you can learn much of her philosophy by what she keeps there. In a wallet inside it she has a page of yellowing paper on which are written words by Abraham Lincoln which describe much of her vision.

You cannot bring about prosperity by discouraging thrift.
You cannot strengthen the weak by weakening the strong.
You cannot help small men by tearing down big men.
You cannot help the wage-earner by pulling down the wage-payer.
You cannot further the brotherhood of man by encouraging class hatred.
You cannot help the poor by destroying the rich.
You cannot establish sound security on borrowed money.
You cannot keep out of trouble by spending more than you earn.

> You cannot build character and courage by taking away man's
> initiative and independence.
> You cannot help men permanently by doing for them what they
> could and should do for themselves.

But even when and if her vision is allowed the time to grow, she has none of the illusions of socialists that this will result in a heaven on earth. She encapsulated her political vision and its practical limitations in March 1980 when speaking to the Conservative Central Council at Bournemouth. It was not, she said, a vision of a utopia.

Utopia is an illusion. We shall never live in a society free from material worries. We shall never live in a land which will flow with milk and honey, regardless of our skill and industry.

The better and stronger Britain towards which we in the Government are striving is not a utopia. It's a land in which individuals will have a fair chance, by their own efforts, of winning happiness and security for themselves and their children and, in the process, enlarging the wealth and strength of their country.

Life in that kind of Britain won't be easy. It was not easy for our parents even at the best of times, for they had, by their own hard work and foresight, to do much that, today, is done for us by the State.

I passionately believe in a gradual and orderly return to this kind of personal responsibility – responsibility for the family, to the community, to our country – not because it is the only way to create material wealth – though it is – but because it is the only way to give life dignity and meaning and self-respect.

It is only a society like this, based on individual effort and opportunity, which will ever achieve sufficient wealth to care properly for those in real need.

Socialism has tried – and, in the early days, tried genuinely and with true compassion – to do this. It failed because the system it operated couldn't create the wealth necessary to cure the very social ills that gave it birth.

But if you ask 'Will it be two years or ten before our policies have solved our economic problems?' I have to tell you that no country ever solves all its economic problems.

We shall never be able simply to sit back, free from responsibility, free from the need to work, free from the duty of caring, and just enjoy the fruits of an automated industry. Even if we could, how many of us would find fulfilment in such an existence?

While Utopia must remain forever out of reach, there is one part of her vision that is nearer at hand: an end to the tyranny of the majority by minority groups. It was to these would-be tyrants that Margaret Thatcher turned her attention in a speech to the Carlton Club, in London's St. James's, in 1984. I know from her own off-the-cuff remarks just how much she detests undemocratic pressure groups who try to foist their views on to an unwilling and sometimes unaware majority. This extract from her speech shows just why she is regarded as such an enemy by so many 'politically' based special interest groups, including hard left trade unionists, militant left-wing manipulators of local government, and some intellectual and artistic pressure groups. The speech centred around the need to provide 'protection of the majority'. She explained:

There has come into existence a fashionable view, convenient to many special-interest groups, that there is no need to accept the verdict of the majority: that the minority should be quite free to bully, even coerce, to get the verdict reversed.

Marxists, of course, always had an excuse when they were outvoted: their opponents must have 'false consciousness'; their views did not really count. But the Marxists, as usual, only provide a bogus intellectual top-dressing for groups who seek only their own self-interest.

Plenty of groups operate more simply. They don't care whether they have persuaded their fellow citizens or not, or whether constitutionally elected governments undertake properly approved policies. These minorities will coerce the system to meet their own objectives if we let them get away with it.

Most of the new 'campaigning' pressure groups, run by professionals who move from campaign to campaign – some in the trade unions, some even in parts of the system of Government itself – have seen how our democracy has evolved rules to temper the power of the majority and provide safeguards and rights for the minority. They have spotted that, if minorities bend the rules or simply ignore them, they may succeed in manipulating the whole system. The minority indeed may in the end effectively coerce the majority. . . .

At the time she made this speech, of course, Arthur Scargill was trying to spread throughout the country the strike by the National Union of Mineworkers. His challenge went to the very basis of the rule of law and Parliament and her response in the later part of this speech was aimed at him and those who supported him. It was also directed to those in the country – and even in her Party and Government – who were urging her to reach a consensus and end the strike. This is what she said:

> Now I hope I won't be thought too provocative if I complain again about the sloppy use of the word 'consensus' in such cases. If there is a national debate and a constitutional vote about some matter, and if a recalcitrant minority says 'the vote be damned, we are going to do our level best to stop the majority having its way' then it's no good saying 'we must seek consensus, we must negotiate'. Such a group will never consent, whatever the majority thinks, until it gets what it wants. That is when we have to stand up and be counted; that is when we have to do what we believe to be right.
>
> We must never give in to the oldest and least democratic trick of all – the coercion of the many by the ruthless manipulating few. As soon as we surrender the basic rule which says we must persuade our fellow citizens, not coerce them, then we have joined the ranks of the enemies of democracy.
>
> Now that democracy has been won, it is not heroic to flout the law of the land as if we still struggled in a quagmire where civilisation had yet to be built.
>
> The concept of fair play – a British way of saying 'respect for the rules' – must not be used to allow the minority to overbear the tolerant majority.

Her vision of the type of country she wants is one that she believes the vast majority of her fellow countrymen share. It would have been arrogant to suggest in the early 1980s that she represented the instincts of the nation. But her record in General Elections allows the claim to be made now with some justification.

Men such as Ian Gow, formerly her Parliamentary Private Secretary, would marvel at her instinctive understanding of what most Britons felt, a gut instinct that many – too many – Conservative politicians have not enjoyed. It is that instinct which her critics, usually those from public schools and the upper classes, jeer at as middle-class values, the values perhaps more accurately described as those of Grantham and Finchley. What they failed to recognise in the early days of her Government was that, just as the vast majority of Americans subscribe to the Great American Dream of the boy from the log cabin who becomes President, so most of those in Britain who are middle class identify happily with Margaret Thatcher – and many of those who are not yet middle class want to be middle class.

The themes of instinct and nationhood occur frequently in her speeches. Her vision and what she believes to be the instinct of the British are inextricably intertwined. 'If we cannot trust the deepest instincts of our people, we should not be in politics at all,' she told the 1980 Conservative Party Conference in Brighton. She went on: 'If our people feel that they are part of a great nation and they are prepared to will the means to keep it great, a great nation we shall be and shall remain.' Three years later, after her second General Election victory, she was claiming to have found the very heart of the British people when she said:

> What I think we discovered and expressed, both in our four years of Government and in the programme which grew out of those four years, was where the heart of the British people lies. We are a mature nation which through centuries of trial, sorrow and achievement has developed a common view of life. There are things for which we as a people have stood for centuries:
>
> the will and capacity to defend our way of life;
> the rule of law;
> the belief in private property and home ownership;
> the protection of the elderly and the sick;
> the limitation of Government;
> and the freedom of the individual.

By giving voice to these convictions and by holding fast to them, she believed the whole course of British politics had been altered for at least a generation.

We have created the new common ground and that is why our opponents have been forced to shift their ground. Both the policy and direction of State socialism on which they have been fighting for years have been utterly rejected by our people. State socialism is not in the character of the British people. It has no place in our traditions. It has no hold on our hearts.

We have entered a new era. The Conservative Party has staked out the common ground and the other parties are tiptoeing on to it.

With the benefit of hindsight and a few words that she let slip after the 1987 General Election, it can be seen that Margaret Thatcher invested all her faith in 1979 in what she believed was the real character of the British people. She staked her entire political and personal future on a belief that essentially the British remain today what they were one, three or even five centuries ago. In the mid 1980s productivity rose, and with it industrial output and economic growth until Britain was the fastest-growing economy in Europe with the longest period of positive growth since the Second World War. And as productivity and output rose, Margaret Thatcher had her proof that her faith had not been misplaced.

That third General Election victory, preceded by the long-running surge in production, provided the foundation for the extension of Thatcherism throughout the world. In public, her view is that how other countries run their economies is very much their own business. In private, she is delighted that Thatcherism is helping to put socialism to flight internationally, and her vision is of a steady spread through other countries of the basic economic principles upon which she has operated in the United Kingdom. In fact, Thatcherism has become one of Britain's greatest exports and representatives of countries throughout the world, including both France and Japan, have beaten a path to the door of the British Treasury to learn how to sell off their State assets.

Once, early in her years at Number 10, she remarked that of course Britain would never have another empire – but she seemed to leave her words hanging half-finished in the air. She may perhaps have had a notion of the spreading out from Britain of new ideas, just as the British Empire extended its influence in the past.

Putting on a brave face. Margaret Thatcher welcomed by a Royal Marines' Band in Finchley on the day she knew the troops would land in the Falklands

Margaret Thatcher loves planting trees – but this was a special one planted at Mill Hill Barracks to commemorate Falkland heroes

A warm Falklands welcome from these British troops. *Crown Copyright Reserved*

Margaret Thatcher is always happy with children, and these Falkland Islands'
children are very happy with her. *Crown Copyright Reserved*

Margaret Thatcher visiting the troops in Northern Ireland

The Grand Hotel after the Brighton Bomb and (opposite) being re-opened by Margaret Thatcher – 'Terrorism will never win'

The Queen and Margaret Thatcher with five ex-Prime Ministers at an anniversary dinner in Downing Street

First among equals – the 1988 Cabinet

United in partnership for peace

'He is a man I can do business with'

George Bush gets a warm welcome at Number 10

By 1988 socialism was in retreat round the world. She told the Conservative Central Council in Buxton in March of that year that her policies were now being copied round the world – and not only under Conservative governments.

Other countries' socialists know a good thing when they see one. They are cutting taxes and privatising industries in socialist Australia, in socialist New Zealand and in socialist Spain. And if *perestroika* keeps on rolling along, we might be able to point to even more surprising converts.

In May 1988 she pointed out in a speech to the Conservative Women's national conference:

Other governments – and other socialist governments – are now coming here to see how it is done and to try it out back home. Foreign countries may take their cuisine from Paris, but they take their economics from London. Two weeks ago the Finance Minister in New Zealand's Labour Government was speaking in London. Let me quote you his exact words:

'Our policies, especially in the economic field, do not at first sight look like the policies of a socialist government. Traditional socialist governments do not deregulate banks, cut taxes, sell State-owned assets, remove subsidies or deregulate local industry and free up import access. So why have we done it? The reason is very simple. It is because this Government is more interested in results than in process.'

Interested in results – but how did he know that these policies would achieve the right results? He and other governments knew that these policies worked only because we had the courage to pioneer them, because we believed in them.

We worked hard to achieve our present success. But we can't take it for granted. We still have much to do. We are only in our third term. And a woman's work is never done.

'No one of my generation can forget that America has been the principal architect of a peace in Europe which has lasted forty years.'

(Margaret Thatcher)

12

HER SPECIAL RELATIONSHIP

THERE ARE TWO words that can enervate Margaret Thatcher, bring her to the edge of her chair or put a sparkle of especial interest in her face. Those words are 'United States'. That nation is the nearest to the ideal that Margaret Thatcher would like Britain to emulate. She will be the first, of course, to explain and appreciate that all nations are unique and that she does not want the United Kingdom to become a miniature America. But the sheer rushing, gushing spirit of free enterprise in the United States will always reinforce her own vision for Britain.

There is also something of the American frontier woman about Margaret Thatcher. She draws deeply on the experience of America to derive lessons for Britain today. Her visits to the United States serve to reinvigorate her belief in capitalism, individual enterprise and liberty. An aide who has frequently travelled there with her on official visits recalled that working for her on her return is particularly demanding. 'It's as if going to America recharges her batteries and sets her off in an even more radical direction,' he said.

Every year a young American student arrives to work for Margaret Thatcher in her constituency office in Finchley. The student visits are run by an organisation founded by three ex-Conservative Party agents, but the visitors are selected without regard to whether they are Republican or Democrat by inclination. So an American student who is a Republican could find himself or herself in the office of Neil Kinnock, and a Democrat could – and sometimes does – end up working with Margaret Thatcher.

The students stay for twelve weeks, and the experience is part of their study of British politics. Among those who went through the Finchley Conservative Association office while I was there were Jeanette Heinz, from the famous baked beans dynasty whose family home in California adjoined that of Ronald Reagan; and Gwen Orlowski, who went back to America to work for the Democrats.

Margaret Thatcher made them all feel at home, whatever their political complexion, but there was one who delighted her especially: Juliane Zieroff. She was writing a project article about her experiences in Finchley and when Margaret Thatcher learned of it she startled the young Republican from California by asking what she saw as the biggest differences between America and Great Britain. Juliane Zieroff told her:

> Well, we have our cheats and rogues in our political system – but by and large we know that both our political parties are for America. Here, in Great Britain, if you will forgive me Prime Minister, you have Members of Parliament who are opposed to the whole system of government in this country – and say so. You have Members of what you call Her Majesty's Opposition who are opposed to Her Majesty. That, Prime Minister, is crackers!

This short exposition from the young American clearly reflected Margaret's own feelings. She has sought since the first day she went into 10 Downing Street to reshape politics so that the values of her Conservative Government become the 'common ground' on which her political opponents would be forced to fight. In the early years of her Government, that target looked beyond reach to the faint-hearts who argued that as Margaret Thatcher took the Conservative Party to the right, the Labour Party would go to the left and thus face Britain with the danger of a hard-left Government. I know that in those early years Ian Gow, then Parliamentary Private Secretary to Margaret Thatcher, argued privately that it would take three General Election victories and three full Parliaments to make achievable for British politics this common ground. His words rang loudly in my memory when Margaret Thatcher addressed her tenth Conservative Party Conference as Prime Minister in 1988. With the Labour Party broken-backed and the Conservative Party consolidating a lead in the opinion polls when, by historic standards, the Opposition should have been ahead, she declared that the Conservative Party had now taken over the common ground of British politics.

Suddenly, the shared political principles that Juliane Zieroff could not see in Britain in 1984 when she came to Finchley appeared to be at hand, and Margaret Thatcher's American Dream, of a Britain where the parties fought over little more than the best way to give capitalism its head, seemed close to fulfilment. As if to give additional credence to Margaret Thatcher's declaration that her Party now occupied the common ground, the Labour Party began openly to discuss abandoning the founding and sacred 'Clause Four' of its constitution which binds and commits it to nationalise virtually every major sector of industry, including all those which Margaret Thatcher has denationalised since 1979.

There are some Conservative MPs who look first to the European Community, then to America. Margaret Thatcher looks first to America, then to the European Community, and that she does so is a reflection of her simple and pragmatic approach to life and politics. For her, the European Community is a wonderful ideal that is in the process of working itself into a reality. America is a reality which today already contains the ideals that the Community will take generations to put into practice: a thrusting free-enterprise system that is unquestioned; a commitment to fighting for freedom that is as yet untested in the Community; and the wherewithal, in the shape of nuclear weapons, to defend its freedoms. Perhaps her approach to the two continents can be summed up in one sentence: 'Why look into the crystal ball when you can read the history book?' The European Community is in so many respects still a crystal ball. It is less than fifty years since many of the nations of today's European Community were under the fascist heel of two countries that today are among its leading members.

The glory and the imperfections of the relationship between the United Kingdom and the USA from Margaret Thatcher's point of view are contained in two of the most emotionally charged episodes of her Premiership: the Falklands conflict and the Brighton bomb. In 1982, President Reagan was prepared to put the interests of Britain on the other side of the Atlantic before his relations with South American neighbours. Without the cooperation of America, it would have been impossible for Britain to have won in the South Atlantic. Yet two years later, in Brighton, she and her Cabinet became victims of a terrorist IRA gang which to this day receives much of its financial support from the pockets of Americans, many of whom naively hand over vast sums to NORAID because the American Government fails to spell out to its people clearly enough that the IRA are terrorists who oppose the principles of freedom and democracy which Britain and America have fought side by side to defend.

For all the imperfections, failures and weaknesses of the special relationship – and Margaret Thatcher has no illusions that it is perfect – her reflex of looking first across the Atlantic can be explained and expressed in an extract from her speech to the Conservative Party Conference in 1981. She would argue that the words are just as true today – and are likely to remain so for many years to come, regardless of how the European Community develops. With that knack of expressing the nub of an argument, she said:

> We cannot defend ourselves, either in this island or in Europe, without a close, effective and warm-hearted alliance with the United States. Our friendship with America rests not only on the memory of common dangers jointly faced and of common ancestors. It rests on respect for the same rule of law and representative democracy. Our purpose must be not just to confirm but to strengthen a friendship which has twice saved us this century. Had it not been for the magnanimity of the United States, Europe would not be free today.

She does not merely recognise that Britain's security still depends today on the willingness of America to provide a nuclear umbrella, she is also willing to state publicly the international equivalent of there being no such thing as a free lunch – or in this case a free umbrella.

> We in Britain cannot honourably shelter under the American nuclear umbrella and simultaneously say to our American friends 'You may defend our homes with your home-based missiles but you may not base those missiles anywhere near our homes.'

The price that Britain must pay for keeping tyranny at bay is high, she says, but it is a price that must be paid if the higher cost of war is not to follow.

Her 'Yankophile' political reflex showed up repeatedly in Finchley: she would always speak favourably of America at each annual general meeting of the Conservative Association. There was not the same reflex so far as the European Community was concerned. It would be America to which she would turn, too, in off-the-cuff remarks or when she summed up at her final Finchley engagement on a Friday. These late-night summaries were almost as much for her own benefit as for the Conservative audience fortunate enough to be on the receiving end. Finchley seemed to be the place where she would focus and organise her thoughts on Britain and the wider world.

She is clearly not going to allow that common ground in America which she now sees growing in Britain to be undermined by creeping socialism in the European Community. Nor is she going to permit the bubbling entrepreneurial spirit and non-interventionist American style of government which is daily reflected more strongly in Great Britain to be corrupted by European Commission bureaucrats. Little wonder, then, that she told the Conservative Party Conference in 1988: 'We have not worked all these years to free Britain from the paralysis of socialism only to see it creep in through the back door of central control and bureaucracy from Brussels.'

[161]

This speech put space between her and the Eurocrats and Euro-crazies who want to rush Britain headlong into European political and economic integration. Her message rankled throughout much of Europe, angered the Euro enthusiasts in her own Party, and raised an eyebrow or two beyond Europe itself. In fact, Margaret Thatcher was displaying an extraordinary consistency, and anyone who knows her views on the European Community was not surprised. As long ago as 1979, only days after she first became Prime Minister, she addressed a Europe Rally. The occasion was one for enthusiasm about the European Community, but she took the opportunity, even then, to warn:

> We insist that the institutions of the European Community are man-aged so that they increase the liberty of the individual throughout our continent. These institutions must not be permitted to dwindle into bureaucracy. Whenever they fail to enlarge freedom, the institutions should be criticised and the balance restored.

If for Margaret Thatcher there remains a special relationship with the United States, then this may be due to some extent to the fact that there was something very special about her relationship with President Reagan. It was significant that she was the only world leader to be invited by President Reagan to attend his final dinner at the White House on 16 November 1988 to make the first formal introduction of his successor, George Bush.

The relations between nations are in part influenced by the personal relationships between their leaders – certainly more so than is generally appreciated. In the case of Margaret Thatcher, her mood and reactions after the first meeting with a national leader will be passed to her close political and Civil Service advisers, some of whom will have been present and witnessed for themselves the personal chemistry, or lack of it. Then, as if this mood had some-how been injected into a small spot in the skin of the Government, it spreads out rapidly, first through Number 10 and the Foreign Office and then into the other branches of Government. As an example, the chemistry would appear to have been right between

Margaret Thatcher and Mikhail Gorbachev. 'I can do business with that man,' she said after their first meeting in London. The burgeoning relationship between Margaret Thatcher and President Reagan was well summed up by a startled but delighted Whitehall official who emerged half-way through the speeches they were addressing to each other at the British Embassy in Washington during her first visit to meet the new President in 1981. Nodding in the direction of the banqueting hall, he said: 'There's a love-in going on in there.'

What is not widely appreciated is *why* Margaret Thatcher and Ronald Reagan got on so well. I believe the answer lies in their backgrounds. Margaret Thatcher, small-town grocer's daughter who became Prime Minister, represents the new Conservative meritocracy. Ronald Reagan, son of a hard-drinking shoe salesman and raised in a two-bedroomed flat in Tampico, Illinois, represents the American meritocracy upon which much of Thatcherism is based. He was not quite the boy who went from a log cabin to the White House, but his journey from Tampico to Washington comes from the same story-book.

Until he was twenty-six, Ronald Reagan was a typical product of a small Midwestern town. He was taught by his mother, Nellie, to read and from an early age showed – like Margaret Thatcher – that he had a retentive memory. But unlike the strict Methodist Alderman Roberts, the father of Ronald Reagan had too great a liking for hard drink. John Reagan was enough of a drunkard to be in and out of work, and the experience left his son Ronald with a lifelong aversion to strong drink. He went to the local Eureka College, a small Christian school, and was President of the Students' Union. He made his first political speech at the age of seventeen during a school strike over the elimination of some classes. The classes were restored, the college president resigned and Ronald Reagan was to describe his first taste of politics as 'heady wine'.

He wanted to be an actor, but could not find a job and so became a sportscaster. Then in 1937 – when Margaret Roberts was eleven and going off to Kesteven and Grantham Girls' Grammar School –

he went to Hollywood, and at the age of twenty-six made the first of 51 pictures. When he came out of the American Air Corps in 1946, Margaret Roberts was up at Oxford.

His political career took off in 1964 – by which time Margaret Thatcher was fighting Finchley for the second time in her political career – with a televised speech on behalf of Barry Goldwater's presidential candidacy. The Reagan speech is still seen as one of the few bright spots in an otherwise disastrous Goldwater campaign. The dollars piled in for the Republicans after Ronald Reagan declared to the national TV audience: 'We stand here on the only island of freedom that is left in the whole world. There is no place to flee, no place to escape to. We defend freedom here or it is gone.' A little over-dramatic perhaps, and possibly a little overstated. But it found the heart (and the wallet) of America. Ronald Reagan had demonstrated that he could find the pulse of the nation.

It was to be fifteen years before Margaret Thatcher was to begin to demonstrate that same ability with the British. In 1965, as Ronald Reagan was in the run-up to his election for the first time in 1966 as Governor of California and was being tipped as a future President, Margaret Thatcher was on her way to Washington. He was by then a national name in America. She was a Conservative MP of five years' standing who was scarcely known in her home country, let alone in America. Her visit was paid for by the American Government and she travelled on the International Visitors' Program, leaving on 20 February and returning on 25 March 1965. She spent the first week in Washington seeing at first hand its politics and administration. Then, like the thousands of others on the Program, she spent the next five weeks seeing how ordinary Americans live. Under the Visitors' Program there is no hotel accommodation or limousines – just trains, Greyhound buses and life within a typical American family.

The American Embassy in London keeps scrupulous records of the itinerary of British politicians who have been on the Program. However, in the case of Margaret Thatcher, the file is virtually empty. There is no record of the states she visited or the families with whom she stayed – beyond a note that she visited Montclair in

New Jersey. That trip was an essential stop after Washington for Margaret Thatcher: Montclair is 'twinned' with the Borough of Barnet in which her Finchley constituency lies.

What these two politicians from small towns and humble origins developed was an especially close personal relationship which itself was an important part of the transatlantic special relationship. Its existence was emphasised in the comments of one of Margaret Thatcher's aides in the summer before the 1988 Presidential elections. It is a strict rule of all British Governments that they do not interfere in another country's democratic elections nor ever make any public remarks that might be construed as supporting one candidate against the other. It is because of that rule that only now, after the 1988 elections, can the comments of the aide be recounted.

At this time Governor Dukakis had a clear lead over George Bush in the opinion polls. Bush had yet to launch his campaign, but such was the size of the Dukakis lead that it seemed doubtful that the then American Vice President could convincingly overtake the Democrat candidate. The size of the Dukakis lead in the opinion polls had put the British Prime Minister into a despondent mood and she was beginning to think that she might have to look increasingly across the Channel to the European Community rather than across the Atlantic. 'The trouble is,' said the aide, 'that she feels she can do business with George Bush, but not with Dukakis.' Significantly, the aide went on: 'The special relationship is not merely a relationship between the two countries. Margaret Thatcher sees it very much as a personal relationship between herself and Ronald Reagan.' She had already met with George Bush as Vice President and been impressed, speaking privately with her Downing Street staff later about the likelihood and wisdom of his becoming the Republican candidate for the Presidency in 1988.

Lest it should appear that the relationship between the two political giants of the Western Alliance is based entirely on personalities, it is worth recalling President Reagan's words when he flew into London immediately after his Kremlin summit in 1988. He said that Margaret Thatcher's leadership and the vision of the

British people had been an inspiration to Americans and to all those who love freedom and yearn for peace. In short, the appeal lay in the ability of each of those leaders to demonstrate in political style and policy what the other saw as the finest qualities and traditions of his or her nation.

For George Bush, the eight-year Reagan Presidency is a hard act to follow in terms of relations with Margaret Thatcher. As he sets out on this task after his inauguration, his likelihood of succeeding lies in the fact that Margaret Thatcher sees in him the same qualities that she believes represent America at its finest. Her belief in Bush was caught up by the Young Conservatives at the end of her tenth Party Conference as Prime Minister in 1988. The conference hall was full of blue and white banners emblazoned: 'Thatcher and Bush: the Dream Ticket'.

The best of the British nation was represented by President Reagan's opening words to Margaret Thatcher in London's fifteenth-century Guildhall, after his Kremlin summit: 'From the Marne to El Alamein, to Arnhem, to the Falklands, you have in this century so often remained steadfast for what is right – and against what is wrong. You are a brave people and this land truly is, as your majestic, moving hymn proclaims, a land of hope and glory.'

In return, the best of America and of the special relationship between the two nations was encapsulated in Margaret Thatcher's speech to a joint meeting of the United States Congress in 1985 – a rare privilege for any world leader. She began by recalling that Winston Churchill had been called three times to address a joint meeting of Congress and that each occasion had served as a lamp along a dark road which the British and American people had trod together. But each of those lamps also told a story which later generations in both America and the United Kingdom sometimes found hard to grasp: why past associations bind the two nations so closely. She went on:

No one of my generation can forget that America has been the principal architect of a peace in Europe which has lasted forty years. Given this shield of the United States, we have been granted the opportunities to build a concept of Europe beyond the dreams of our fathers: a Europe which seemed unattainable amid the mud and slaughter of the First World War and the suffering and sacrifice of the Second.

When, in the spring of 1945, the guns fell silent, General Eisenhower called our soldiers to a service of thanksgiving. In the order of service was the famous prayer of Sir Francis Drake: 'O Lord God, when thou givest to Thy servants to endeavour in great matter, grant us to know that it is not the beginning but the continuing of the same, until it be thoroughly finished, which yieldeth the true glory.'

With Europe now enjoying one of its longest periods without war in all its history, she said, she wanted to recall those words and acknowledge how faithfully America had fulfilled them in the decades that had followed General Eisenhower's prayer. She continued:

For our deliverance from what might have befallen us, I would not have us leave our gratitude to the tributes of history. The debt the free peoples of Europe owe to this nation – generous with its bounty, willing to share its strength, seeking to protect the weak – is incalculable.

The Thatcher–Reagan axis of the eighties will surely be remembered for developing a more robust capitalism and for achieving, by strength and unity in the wider North Atlantic alliance, disarmament treaties with the Soviet Union. Diplomats, businessmen and politicians have all played their part in securing these successes, but the pivot was the personal relationship of Ronald Reagan and Margaret Thatcher.

The British politicians who today have eyes only for the European Community might be inclined upon reading these words to think that Margaret Thatcher would have liked to have been born an American. That is not too far from the truth. For what was largely overlooked when she made that speech were the personal references to Winston Churchill whom, she said, had the 'special advantage' of having blood ties with the country through his American mother. Margaret Thatcher added: 'Alas for me, these are not matters we can readily arrange for ourselves.' However, her son Mark has been able to make up for the lack of American blood so far in the veins of her family. He has not only married an American, but at the time of writing is set to provide her with something more than just the grandchild she longs for: a grandchild who will be American by birth.

'When he stands like an ox in the furrow with his
sullen set eyes on your own
And grumbles "This isn't fair dealing", my son,
leave the Saxon alone'   (Rudyard Kipling)

13

THE FALKLANDS WAR

MARGARET THATCHER wore two very different faces during the Falklands War – one in public, the other in private. The public face is embedded deeply in the nation's memory; her private face is as deeply embedded in my memory. It was a face full of tears.

She was required in public to wear the face of Britain's resolution, determination, ruggedness and patriotism. It is a face that she wears easily, because she is the supreme patriot with a sense of what the ordinary Briton feels about his country.

As mentioned earlier, one of her favourite poems is Rudyard Kipling's 'Norman and Saxon', which is set in AD 1100.

'My son,' said the Norman Baron, 'I am dying, and you will be heir
To all the broad acres in England that William gave me for my share
When we conquered the Saxon at Hastings, and a nice little handful it
   is.
But before you go over to rule it I want you to understand this:
The Saxon is not like us Normans. His manners are not so polite.
But he never means anything serious till he talks about justice and
   right.
When he stands like an ox in the furrow with his sullen set eyes on your
   own
And grumbles "This isn't fair dealing", my son, leave the Saxon alone.'

[171]

When the Argentinian 'scrap dealers' landed in the Falklands in 1982 and General Galtieri followed up with a full-scale invasion of the islands, Margaret Thatcher identified with the Saxon. What had happened to the fellow islanders 8000 miles away in the Falklands, who lived and worked under the British Crown and flag, was simply not just, right or 'fair dealing'. As she put it to the House of Commons as the Task Force prepared to sail:

> The people of the Falkland Islands, like the people of the United Kingdom, are an island race. They are few in number but they have the right to live in peace, to choose their own way of life and to determine their own allegiance. Their way of life is British; their allegiance is to the Crown. It is the wish of the British people and the duty of Her Majesty's Government to do everything that we can to uphold that right.

She now stood like the 'ox in the furrow' and her eyes were set firmly on those of General Galtieri on the other side of the world. In speech after speech she sought to revive and maintain the spirit that had built an empire and kept its enemies at bay for almost a thousand years. She knew that in the new age of mass electronic communications, a wartime leader – for that is what she was for a few weeks – can show no sign of personal weakness in public lest morale be crumbled in fifteen million living rooms by a few seconds of newsreel film on television screens. For despite the initial surge of anger among the British people at the Argentinian invasion, the Cabinet was uncertain how much stomach the nation would have for the fight when the first 'body bags' containing the corpses of British servicemen began to appear on the television screens.

Listening to her in public, it was easy to forget that the effective Commander-in-Chief was a wife and mother. Britain had been called once more, she declared, to stand up for freedom and the rule of law. It was the older generation of Britons and generations before them, she told Conservatives in London, who had made sacrifices so that we could be a free society and belong to a community of nations. Today it fell to the new generation to bear the same responsibility.

[172]

Behind the scenes in the Government and the Conservative Party, it was a different story. The Cabinet was not quite as united in private as it looked in public. Both John Biffen, Trade and Industry Secretary in the first days of the conflict and later Leader of the Commons, and Lord Hailsham, the Lord Chancellor, were notable for their reservations about the Task Force fighting its way to Port Stanley if a diplomatic solution could not be found. And deep within the Conservative Party, contingency plans were being made to deal with the potential domestic political crisis if the Task Force had to be ordered to withdraw and the nation and the Party demanded the resignation of Margaret Thatcher.

With those political forces at her back, unseen by the nation at large, there was no political or rational alternative but for her to see through what instinct in any event told her she must do: recover the Falklands, with the minimum possible loss of life.

Assisted by her own powerful oratory, it was easy for those such as Labour's Tam Dalyell, MP for Linlithgow, to project Margaret Thatcher subsequently as the woman who sank the *Belgrano* without a thought for the loss of life, and who sank with it any chance of a Peruvian-inspired peace deal. Even her exclamation after the first success of the British campaign, when marines recaptured South Georgia 800 miles west of the Falklands, was quickly twisted and misinterpreted by her political opponents. She said 'Rejoice! Rejoice!' and was instantly accused of revelling in warfare. In fact, she was rejoicing that South Georgia had been recaptured without loss of life.

Hoisted by her own patriotic rhetoric, it became easy to depict the first woman Prime Minister as somehow unfeeling, almost inhuman. At best, she seemed to be committed to the idea of putting the Argentinian robber to flight. At worst, she seemed to be giving not so much as a glance towards the human victims of war. In terms of basic presentation, she had a problem. Women are traditionally the bearers and protectors of life, not the hunters and killers. She did her best to cope with this essential contradiction by in public keeping her eyes firmly on the high ground of the morality of nations and international politics, not the humans in the foothills.

[173]

The public face of Margaret Thatcher during the Falklands is perhaps best summed up in her own ringing words when the war was over and won. She said:

> This nation had the resolution to do what it knew had to be done – to do what it knew was right.
>
> We fought to show that aggression does not pay and that the robber cannot be allowed to get away with his swag. We fought with the support of so many throughout the world: the Security Council, the Commonwealth, the European Community, and the United States. Yet we also fought alone – for we fought for our own people and for our own sovereign territory.
>
> Now that it is all over, things cannot be the same again, for we have learned something about ourselves – a lesson which we desperately needed to learn. When we started out, there were the waverers and the faint-hearts. The people who thought that Britain could no longer seize the initiative for herself. The people who thought we could no longer do the great things which we once did. Those who believed that our decline was irreversible – that we could never again be what we were. There were those who would not admit it – even perhaps some here today – people who would have strenuously denied the suggestion but, in their heart of hearts, they too had their secret fears that it was true: that Britain was no longer the nation that had built an Empire and ruled a quarter of the world.
>
> Well they were wrong. The lesson of the Falklands is that Britain has not changed and that this nation still has those sterling qualities which shine through our history. This generation can match their fathers and grandfathers in ability, in courage, and in resolution. We have not changed. When the demands of war and the dangers to our own people call us to arms, then we British are as we have always been.

But if her public face demonstrated stern determination, her private face showed that the human losses of war were as painful for her as for any other mother. The ordeal for her was to superimpose her will and the logistics of war upon her emotions.

It was on 22 May, towards the end of the war, that her private face began to become dangerously visible, during a visit to Finchley. It was a trip that by her standards was long overdue. She had been forced to cancel the previously planned visit, on the

Friday after the invasion, because the Cabinet was meeting in emergency session. It was extraordinary for the Cabinet to meet on a Friday, but almost more extraordinary for Margaret Thatcher to cancel a visit to her constituency. She was therefore particularly reluctant to put off the visit planned for 22 May, and there were special reasons for her insistence on going ahead with it. She was due to open the third phase of a warehouse development, and though that might seem a pedestrian event when there is a war going on, there was for her a particular significance attached to it. She had opened the first phase when she was the new Finchley MP. She had opened the second phase as Leader of the Opposition. Now she wanted to complete the hat-trick in Finchley by opening the third phase as Prime Minister.

She was due in Finchley at noon straight from a meeting of her War Cabinet. One of her Special Branch officers who arrived in advance warned me with some understatement that there had been a 'problem' in the Falklands and that marines had been killed. The news had reached him on his short-wave radio as it was sent to the Prime Minister in her car on the journey from Downing Street. Two helicopters had collided and crashed. At that stage, no one in the country save her, the War Cabinet and the military commanders knew that the retaking of the Falklands was under way, and the collision seemed a fearful augury of massacre, disaster and bloodshed and a death toll beyond the calculations of the Chiefs of Staff.

When she arrived in Finchley, she stepped out of her Daimler wearing a sombre black silk printed dress, black fitted coat, black shoes and dark-coloured tights. But she was also wearing a look of great depression. Denis Thatcher had driven up with her and stayed very close to her all afternoon as if determined to support her physically as well as morally. He is a man of many words, who has succeeded in saying very few in public lest they detract from his wife, and he was giving her all the silent support he could muster that day. She seemed ready to collapse from the sheer weary weight of the awfulness of the war as she walked through the warehouse in front of 600 people. At times, as when HMS

Sheffield was sunk by a single Exocet missile, she looked completely drained of all energy.

On this day, as she walked across the floor of the new warehouse with the news of the loss of the marines still ringing in her ears, there was a moment of dreadful irony and poignancy. A band of the Royal Marines, arranged to launch the ceremony long before the Task Force had been despatched for action, struck up. The Prime Minister froze, and might have remained there for some time had not Denis, whose arm until then had simply provided gentle support, physically pulled her on.

From the platform Michael Gerson, the businessman whose warehouse she had come to open, made his speech and the Prime Minister replied that everyone would understand if she did not take any longer than necessary because all hearts and minds were thousands of miles away. 'It may be the other side of the world,' she said, 'but they are just a heartbeat away.'

The lunch that followed was interrupted three times with messages from Downing Street before she and Denis made their way out and towards the waiting car. As she stood up to leave, every guest rose at their tables. There were about 600 people there but, rather than the usual applause and cheers, it was as if the volume control had been switched off on that floor. Amid this great silence, there were hands waving at her as she made her way out. Denis said, as if to a child: 'Margaret, they are all waving.' She turned round to the forest of hands and again, quietly but firmly, he said: 'Wave back, Margaret. Wave back.' She did so, then climbed into the back of the Daimler. A single flash bulb cracked. I was told that the *Daily Mirror* had the picture but whichever newspaper it was, there was nothing of it in the next morning's editions, much to the relief of the staff at 10 Downing Street. The photograph would have shown the British Prime Minister crying, her face awash with tears as she climbed into the car. On the back of a House of Commons envelope lying on the leather seat were words scribbled down by her after the message had come through about the loss of the helicopters and the marines in them: 'Only a heartbeat away'.

Male political or military leaders who send servicemen into

battle then sleep soundly and eat well are not singled out as uncaring or bloodthirsty. They are performing the role that society has allotted to them. Margaret Thatcher performed that role, as effective Commander-in-Chief of the British armed forces, as well as any man. She did it also as a woman and a mother. Perhaps we are so conditioned as a society to role-play that while it was just acceptable for her to cry when Mark was lost in the Sahara, or to pause to wipe away a tear from the corner of her eye during a televised discussion about her father, morale would have sunk in Britain and in the Task Force if the Prime Minister of Great Britain and Northern Ireland had been pictured breaking down and weeping on 22 May 1982.

The journey back to the Finchley Conservative Association building in Ballards Lane ended with my walking into the office and interrupting a British Telecom engineer in the final stages of installing a scrambler telephone in the office, suddenly an essential piece of equipment. The short youth with heavily tattooed arms was sitting on the floor fixing the final wires. He looked up and said 'Hello sir. Is this for Maggie?' From behind me a voice said 'Yes dear,' and the Prime Minister moved forward to identify herself. The engineer flushed deeply and got up to leave with the look of a man who wished for once that he was even smaller. She fixed him with a smile and said 'Well done, lad.' A moment later, the Special Branch man told me that riots were expected in London that night. When I looked perplexed, he nodded at the British Telecom engineer, now swaggering down the path, and said: 'If anyone says a word about the Prime Minister in the pub tonight, he'll tear them to pieces.'

By this time, her exhaustion was almost complete. She sat down at her desk as usual and, for my part just as routinely, I handed her the constituency file. She began to go through it paper by paper, but just fiddled with them instead of getting stuck in as she had always done. Her mind was exhausted, and it was certainly not in 212 Ballards Lane. I suggested that she did not really want to look at her constituency papers, and for a moment the blue eyes seemed to flash with defiance and be ready to prove me wrong. (Perhaps not so remarkably for her, she had that week while running a war found the time to top and tail a dozen letters to her constituents on issues ranging from Poland to social security.) But then she just said 'No', and in a role that for me was as unusual as it was short-lived, I suggested that what she needed was rest.

I told her firmly that she should go upstairs to the attic where there was a couch and get some sleep. She agreed, and disappeared for an hour and a half. She then came back, make-up freshened and clearly feeling refreshed herself. Suddenly the new scrambler telephone seemed to be in almost constant use and I took myself off, only to be called back as the Prime Minister demanded to be taken quickly to a television. A set on the first floor warmed into life to show the face of John Nott, then Defence Secretary, announcing that he had received a signal from General Jeremy Moore saying that a bridgehead had been established at San Carlos and the Union flag was flying again over the Falklands. For the second time that day the Prime Minister froze, but there was no Denis with her this time and she stayed motionless for a full thirty seconds. Then her whole body came alive again with a huge jerk, as she said: 'That's it! That's what I've been waiting for all day. Let's go!' The bustling, practical Margaret Thatcher was back in action.

It was not to Downing Street that she headed but to Woodhouse School for a farewell party for 400 to mark the retirement of Roy Langstone, my predecessor as Finchley agent, who had arrived in the constituency 22 years earlier, long before Margaret Thatcher was Prime Minister. While that party was going on, a more spontaneous one was gathering behind the crowd control barriers at Number 10 as Britons turned out to catch the first glimpse of Margaret Thatcher since John Nott announced the establishment of the bridgehead. As she arrived back at Number 10, she said: 'We must go and speak to the people.' With that she leant over the crowd control barriers to start shaking the outstretched hands.

After the Argentinians surrendered and the Union flag was once more flying over Port Stanley, it was left to Enoch Powell to pay a huge compliment to Margaret Thatcher, worth that much more as it came from a man who is not easily given to paying them. He said that he had received a copy of a report of the public analyst of a substance recently tested. In an obvious analogy to the Prime Minister, he said: 'It shows that the substance under test consists of ferrous metal of the highest quality. It is of exceptional tensile strength, resistant to wear and tear, and may be used with advantage for all national purposes.' Enoch Powell's unbounded praise is quite well known, but less well publicised was the Iron Lady's reply. After telling him that she was 'very grateful indeed', she added without a shred of modesty: 'I agree with every word he says.'

The Iron Lady had indeed withstood her greatest test, but it had been, as Wellington said after Waterloo, a 'damn close thing'. It had been close for Britain, close for the Task Force and much closer, too, for Margaret Thatcher than she suggested to Enoch Powell that afternoon in the Commons. But by then, of course, the public face was back in place.

'So, sitting in the dark and the silence of the bomb-blasted Brighton bedroom, Margaret Thatcher made a vow to herself: whatever happened to her in the future, she would never again allow herself to be in the clinging darkness.'

14

THE BRIGHTON BOMB

EVERYONE HAS A secret, very private terror. It was a theme of George Orwell's novel *1984*, and in that very year, when the IRA blasted the Grand Hotel at Brighton, Margaret Thatcher found within herself her own secret terror. A dread of the dark remains a legacy of the events in Brighton in the early hours of that October Friday.

The bomb which was planted in the Grand Hotel exploded at 2.54 a.m. on 12 October, shortly after I had left the hotel in a taxi, one of the last to leave after an evening that had begun with a round of receptions, including the Conference Ball, and ended in the hotel's bar. The taxi took me back to my hotel in Hove, where a little over three hours later a phone call from Sue Thurlow, wife of the Finchley Constituency Association Chairman, broke the news that the IRA had tried to blow into eternity Margaret Thatcher and the majority of her Cabinet, and had come within a whisker of their ambition. The miracle to anyone looking at the Grand Hotel in the early morning light was that they had not succeeded. The front of the hotel, which had always looked like a tall and fancily iced cake, had been sliced away as if by a huge knife. With some of the five who did die still unaccounted for, and Norman Tebbit and John Wakeham being lifted from the debris to be taken to hospital,

[183]

everyone from the Party in Brighton that morning knew without the need for discussion that the Conference had to go to the end of its final day. Without having to be told, the thousands of Conservatives made their way to the conference hall. In all the hotels that morning, the Conservatives knew that Margaret would be there. The IRA could not be given the prize of a foreshortened Conference as evidence that they could disrupt Great Britain's political system.

In times of crisis, Margaret Thatcher is at her best. She has said, as if to dismiss her abundant capacity to cope, that all women and mothers have to contend with multifarious problems, all apparently needing attention simultaneously. But the process of simply getting on with life in a crisis does have a side effect: the personal trauma gets bottled up. Eventually the great unburdening has to take place, though with Margaret Thatcher it was not until some time after the event that this happened. That day in Brighton she acted with dignity and courage, and the subsequent round of apparently endless hospital visits to the injured showed again that punctilious correctness which is one of her traits.

The visible proof for me that life with Margaret Thatcher was never going to be the same after Brighton came with her next call to Finchley on the following Saturday. The complement of armed Special Branch men was trebled, and when a Chief Superintendent arrived to investigate the security risks attached to a planned visit to St Michael's Convent School, he announced that he was closing all the roads in the area. I warned that he would upset the Prime Minister if he started closing roads for her. He said: 'OK, then we'll just have to upset her.' There was a particularly sad note to the descent of the vast security net that Saturday: Margaret Thatcher was visiting her constituency to celebrate her twenty-five years as its Member of Parliament.

Part of her style as Prime Minister is her resistance to all security measures which single her out as special. She finds the security 'hype' of many foreign countries fascinating to behold but quite out of keeping with the Britain she remembers and wants re-established. After Brighton, however, it had to change. Policemen appeared on rooftops, the security firm employed by Conservative Central Office in London was used for functions in Finchley, and an electronic security system was installed at the constituency Conservative Association office. It was here that the dam that had held back her feelings finally burst.

Quite what prompted the outpouring has never been clear. She was sitting in the first-floor room after completing a charity function where she had handed over a £2000 cheque for the Army Benevolent Fund. Around her in the Conservative office were a dozen friends, officers from the Association and, of course, the Special Branch men who had become so much more important a part of her life since Brighton. It was 5.20 p.m. and the general flow of conversation suddenly threw up the word 'Brighton'. Until then, the subject had been either carefully avoided or busily sidestepped by Margaret Thatcher with her knack of deftly changing the subject. But that afternoon it was as if a nerve in her had been struck. A Special Branch officer there at the time remarked later that she had never before spoken with such personal feeling or detail about that early morning in the Grand Hotel.

It was in the parish church at Chequers two days after she had returned from what remained of the Grand Hotel that the sunlight falling through a stained-glass window on to the flowers in the church had suddenly brought home to her the realisation that she had not been meant by the IRA to see that day. Now, at Finchley, she kicked off her black court shoes and unleashed just under thirty minutes of intense although at times halting recollections.

She recalled how in the early hours she and Denis had returned to their suite at the hotel. She had been working into the early hours with Party Chairman John Selwyn Gummer on her keynote end-of-Conference speech. It was not unusual for her to work so late on a speech, but after it was completed she had continued with yet more work – this time urgent Government papers handed to her by Robin Butler, her Principal Private Secretary, in the drawing room of the hotel suite. Then she had taken off her suit and laid it over the back of the settee. 'That was very naughty,' she said. The words 'very naughty' seemed to jar with everyone else in the room. It was so unlike the Prime Minister to use a childish word to describe such an event. In fact, it had been because she had broken her own rule in the early hours of that morning that she had known just where to find her clothes immediately after the bomb exploded, the masonry crashed and the power went off. (She had also found two shirts for Denis, she said.)

In the next room had been Penny Gummer, wife of John. Penny had put a hand round the back of the bathroom door and brought her dressing-gown into the bedroom with her. A week later she had returned in the daylight to Brighton and what remained of the hotel. She had seen that the bathroom itself had been blown away and that she would have plunged to her death if she had tried to walk on the bathroom floor, for it was no longer there. Recounting this part of the story seemed to affect Margaret Thatcher greatly, perhaps because it illustrated the inches and seconds that had made the difference between life and death for herself and Denis, as well as for Penny Gummer.

The reliving by the Prime Minister of her moments in the suite seemed to make her oblivious to all who were with her in the room at Finchley. Speaking seemed to act as some sort of catharsis. Her voice, usually so confident and flowing, was broken. The sentences came in bursts, the pauses were unnaturally long. Not once did she look at anyone else; the eye contact which she uses in company had vanished. She was looking not at us but into thin air. For some of those present, it was an embarrassment. One said later that it was as discomfiting as watching someone undress in public.

It was the darkness that had affected her most in the bedroom after the bomb, she said. She and Denis had been forced to sit in the dark and wait, motionless. From the distance, the voice of a Special Branch officer had ordered them not to move, to stay quite still in case there was a second bomb or an IRA sniper. A figure had been spotted on a nearby rooftop and her security men were taking no chances. Still she had to sit in that enveloping darkness, unmoving and listening for the voices of her distant guards. By chance, one of the first rescue ladders rested against her balcony. But still the Special Branch shouted for her not to move, to stay where she was in the dark. They feared that she would be the target for an IRA bullet that might succeed where the bomb had failed. So, sitting in the dark and the silence of the bomb-blasted Brighton bedroom, Margaret Thatcher made a vow to herself: whatever happened to her in future, she would never again allow herself to be in the clinging darkness.

Then, at the rear of what was left of the Grand Hotel, her Daimler and a police van drew up to take her, Denis and Cabinet colleagues to Brighton police station, the nearest place that the Special Branch were satisfied could be turned into a fortress. With her security guards finally shouting for her to move and leave the darkness, she grabbed two clean blouses, shoes and two cases – one containing Cabinet papers and the other her make-up. Hurrying down to the car, she bumped into fireman Dave Norris and, with fastidious correctness even at such a moment, said 'Good morning, pleased to see you.'

Subsequently, when Margaret Thatcher was on a visit to the United States, a high-ranking American naval officer found himself talking to the British Prime Minister at an official dinner. She told him that she would like to visit Pearl Harbor. The officer said he would be delighted to take her there that very night, were it not for the fact that it was so dark. To his astonishment, she said that they could indeed see the harbour that night. The darkness was no problem, she said, and opened her handbag to produce a torch. She explained: 'I always carry a torch in my handbag, since Brighton.'

The Brighton bomb also brought her much closer to her Special Branch guards, who have become truly special to her. A frequent question to those who have worked with Margaret Thatcher is how she gets on with her staff, as if the questioner half expects that she is insatiably demanding or ferociously bad-tempered. The truth is that there is nothing special about her relationships with most employees, save for the Special Branch. Her liking for these plain-clothes men who guard her is part of a wider love of the armed forces, the police, and any group which, in or out of uniform, is disciplined and protective.

The treatment by Cabinet Ministers of the Special Branch men varies considerably and, as with Government chauffeurs, talk of the kindnesses or indiscretions of individual Ministers soon travels through their ranks, swapped over cups of tea in canteens. The behaviour of a Minister towards his or her chauffeur or Special Branch officer may not tell much about his or her ability as a politician and administrator, but it does reveal a lot about that person as a member of the human race. For instance, it was known by Government chauffeurs long before it became widely known that Dr David Owen had a tendency towards arrogance. In fact, at one time when he was Foreign Secretary there was a crisis in Whitehall because no one came forward to be his driver. Similarly, it is known to the Special Branch which Cabinet Minister left his protectors sitting outside all Christmas Day without so much as the offer of a mince pie.

The public sees little of the security surrounding the Prime Minister, even today. This is in keeping with her wish to avoid as much as possible overt displays of protection, as well as with the wishes of the Special Branch and police. She will be seen, photographed and filmed while she speaks from rostrums, arrives and leaves. But the men almost constantly a stride from her side try to remain out of camera view. She spends many hours each day in the company of these men, one of whom has repeatedly declined promotion to stay at her side. A car drive from 10 Downing Street to a corner of the kingdom will mean the Prime Minister closeted with the driver, an armed Special Branch officer, and a Garden Girl secretary.

The relationship between Prime Minister and guards could have developed in one of two ways – with her regarding the men as pieces of moving furniture, or with her treating them as people. They are very much people, and if a Special Branch man leaves 10 Downing Street she will rearrange her diary appointments to switch Ministers and statesmen around in her programme to try to attend the farewell drinks party. It is not that the relationship between her and the Special Branch is over-friendly, but the Brighton bomb brought home in very real terms something which she had always known in theory: that the guards are what stand between her and men like those who killed her close personal and political friend Airey Neave two months before the 1979 General Election. Increasingly after Brighton, she would seek out their company. Given the choice between eating a salad alone at her desk in the Finchley Conservative Association office and going upstairs to eat with the Special Branch men, she would go upstairs. Her arrival would change the atmosphere, but not to one of formality. The more colourful jokes would stop, as would the ribbing of the Garden Girl secretary.

She calls them 'the boys', and they are in easy company together. For her, 'the boys' are a channel of news about Denis. How will he be getting to Chequers? The Special Branch will know. Will she be seeing him at the engagements tomorrow night? The Special Branch will tell her.

Protecting the Prime Minister has its perks, which are obviously sufficient to compensate a man such as Detective Constable Kingston when he refuses promotion. Some of the power and the glory inevitably rubs off. So, it is still worth something more than a promotion to sergeant and a pay rise for a member of her security staff to listen to a uniformed Chief Superintendent tell him how security at an event is going to be organised, then draw himself up to his full Detective Constable's rank, give his own alternative opinion, and watch the mighty rank of Chief Superintendent crumble. As with so much that concerns the office of Prime Minister, the power is not officially defined. It is just that you do not lightly argue with a man specially charged with protecting the Prime Minister.

It was necessary to be in Finchley for only a few days as agent for the full weight of the security men around the Prime Minister to be felt. Before she goes anywhere on an engagement, even in her constituency, the Special Branch carry out an 'advancement' – a dry run designed to anticipate every conceivable problem and threat. The first advancement with which I was involved found me sitting in the Prime Minister's Daimler as it covered the planned route, with a Special Branch officer chatting about the car phone, how it worked and how to use it. It was something of a dream world for the new agent, who felt like an eight-year-old sitting in a Concorde flight deck. The Special Branch man said: 'You're not taking this in, are you?' – but it seemed foolish to agree that most of what he had said had gone straight over my head. As the Daimler stopped, he called for an explanation of how to work the phone, which bears little relation to the standard British Telecom issue. I began to try, faltered and failed. He pointed through the windscreen to the door through which the Prime Minister was going to walk on the coming Friday, and snarled: 'So if I come down those steps holding her shot and bleeding in my arms, are you going to get out of this car and go off to find a phone box?' After that, he needed to explain the instructions only once more.

There is also something about any elite group which sets it apart, and it was that very eliteness of the Special Branch that made Sir Kenneth Newman when he was first Metropolitan Police Commissioner question and threaten to disband the group. Word quickly reached the Special Branch at Number 10 that Sir Kenneth was being urged by some of his advisers to scrap them on the grounds that they were too much of a 'force within the Force'. The sympathy which Sir Kenneth appeared to be expressing with the idea of disbanding the Special Branch led me to suggest to one security officer at 10 Downing Street that he was in the best position to do something to stop it. 'That's just the problem,' he said. 'We can hardly take the issue up with her when she is sitting in the back of the car. It's just not on to say conversationally to the Prime Minister, "Oh, by the way, had you heard that Scotland Yard is thinking of doing away with us?"'

A month later the same Special Branch officer told me: 'Neither I nor the other officers needed to raise the subject with the Prime Minister. She raised the future of the Special Branch with us.' She had broached the subject in her Daimler when a Special Branch Chief Inspector had been riding shotgun in the passenger seat of her car. Sitting behind him, she had announced that she was aware that proposals to abolish the Special Branch were under discussion. But, added the Prime Minister, it would not happen. Nor did it.

There is one rider that needs to be added to the relationship between Margaret Thatcher and 'the boys'. Strong though their affinity became after the Brighton bomb, this was born more out of having a shared enemy than from fear. She had known long before October 1984 that she was at the top of the IRA's assassination list – everyone at the top in political life realises the risks they run. The risks become even more apparent if you are a prominent member of the Cabinet who wakes up one morning to find that the familiar Special Branch man has gone and that a member of the Special Air Service has taken his place.

Immediately after the bombing of the Grand Hotel, the IRA said in a statement that Margaret Thatcher had been lucky, and needed to be lucky all the time; they had to be lucky only once. It was said to me by someone who watched her closely after October 1984 that there was on occasion a fear in her eyes as she stepped in and out of her Daimler. Perhaps. Much depends on the eye of the beholder, and for my part there seemed after her third General Election victory to be something more serene about her when she was at the moments of greatest personal risk, as if she senses now that, even if the IRA secured their target of assassinating her, it is no longer remotely conceivable that her death could have the result they would wish for. Of course, part of the IRA's strategy is to create the circumstances in which the right wing of the Conservative Party and the Unionist forces in Ulster will lash back so hard that the conditions will be created in Northern Ireland for a small Lebanon or Vietnam. Ironically for the IRA, she is now too big a national and international figure for her assassination to achieve that aim. The backlash against them would come from both sides of the Atlantic and would remove for generations to come the last, flimsy doubts in the minds of the uninformed who equate the IRA with Irish nationalism rather than vicious terrorism.

'While her mind is totally engaged in conversation, her body will succumb and her other hand will lift from passing plates cakes, sponges and other fattening treats.'

15

LIKES AND DISLIKES

ESSENTIALLY Margaret Thatcher is a straightforward woman who provides simple solutions to what many others believe to be complicated problems. Her tastes are equally simple.

The food and drink that politicians order when someone else is paying can be quite revealing about their characters and general philosophies of life. Some members of Labour's Shadow Cabinet are prone to order the most expensive items on the restaurant menu and sniff their host into the more refined zones of the wine list, while members of the Conservative Cabinet show a surprising appetite for omelettes, mixed grills and simple claret.

Margaret Thatcher is among those with simple tastes in food and wine. She has no pretensions with food; in her deep freeze in the flat at 10 Downing Street can usually be found lasagne, mince and shepherd's pies. Her favourite wines are English, usually from Kent, and she asks for them to be served at Chequers when she is entertaining. A favourite menu is: prawn cocktail, with lasagne as a main course, followed by lemon mousse.

Even such a menu overstates the sophistication of her tastes. For twenty-five years she has been going to the old people's party held on Finchley's Grange Estate and organised by Old People's Welfare. Every year the stubborn, independent octagenarians

[195]

gather for a meal which invariably comprises tomato soup followed by tinned potatoes and tinned meat. It is not difficult when
watching someone eat to detect feigned enthusiasm. When Margaret Thatcher sits down to dine with the old folk, there is no doubt
how she feels about the menu. She sets about her meal as if she had
been looking forward to it all year. The paper plates seem only to
increase the pleasures of the tinned food.

Her love of lasagne is born of a still greater love of plain mince
which, given the choice, she would opt for. Lemon mousse as a
favourite dessert is a little deceptive, too. If she were eating alone
and could choose her own favourite, this would be insufficiently
sugary or rich for her very sweet tooth. Something with lots of
syrup or cream poured over the top is most toothsome to the Prime
Minister, though she does not admit to it easily.

If she is to be a guest at an afternoon function, enquiries may well
be made in advance by the hosts about what should be served. The
hostess will be told by Downing Street staff that Margaret wishes
that only tea be served to her. (She takes it without sugar.)
However, as the function gets under way and the afternoon draws
on, the Prime Minister will settle down with her cup of tea held
unfailingly unspilled in her left hand and as the cream buns pass by
will find herself overcome by temptation. While her mind is totally
engaged in conversation, her body will succumb and her other
hand will lift from passing plates cakes, sponges and other fattening treats.

She was once asked to name her favourite dessert and gave
instructions to me to find the recipe for 'Scotch pancakes'. (The
'Scotch' jarred somewhat, because she meant 'Scottish'.) What she
had in mind was a quarter-inch-thick muffin cooked on a griddle
and served with layers of butter, jam and cream. Her delight in
sweet, sticky foods may go back to a childhood from which they
were largely absent; the home of Alderman Roberts followed an
austere regime. Whatever the cause of her attraction to these
fattening foods, their effects will soon be lost. She seems able to
lose weight almost as quickly as it is put on. She can lose a stone in
weight inside a month. At formal dinners and lunches she is

inclined to pick at her food, partly because the sauces are too rich for her taste and partly because she has disciplined herself, much as the Queen does, to make a practice of not consuming all of each dish that is set before her on formal occasions.

For breakfast she likes a cup of black coffee and a vitamin C tablet (though the tablet is a comparatively recent innovation). She used to eat an apple for breakfast, and its disappearance coincided with the capping of her front teeth when she became Leader of the Conservative Party and media advisers moved in. She likes a large glass of scotch and soda in the evening, but dislikes people who drink to excess. One Minister who drank too much at a Downing Street reception lost his job shortly afterwards.

For relaxation, she likes interior do-it-yourself. A cynical nation may be suspicious of photographs of the Prime Minister up a ladder, believing that her enthusiasm lasts only as long as the flash bulbs. In fact, interior decorating is a genuine relaxation. At the end of 1983, after her second General Election win and a tough week, she was asked one Friday in Finchley: 'Are you going to have a quiet day tomorrow?' She said that she was going to paint and paper her daughter Carol's flat. The disbelief must have shown on my face because she insisted later: 'I love it – decorating is a wonderful way to relax.' The decorating that day was more than practical. Carol had been low in spirits, and her mother's way of helping takes the form of busy activity. Sitting around and moping has never been part of her therapy, for herself or for others.

She likes photographs of herself and once in Finchley expressed regret that she had never learned to use a camera. Subsequently, and on the advice of her daughter Carol, the Finchley dining club presented her with a Japanese fully automatic camera. Today one of her preferred leisure activities is taking photographs with it.

She likes the company of men. To say that she dislikes the company of women is to make a black and white issue out of something that has shades. But faced at a function with a group of men and women, she will instinctively turn to the men – and it seems always to have been so. Even at Oxford it was noticed that she preferred to seek out male company. It is not that she is ever rude to women; she is simply more enthused by the company of men. Having worked for so long in the predominantly male world of Westminster, she turns out of habit to men rather than women, as on one particular afternoon on the terrace at the House of Commons when she walked out to meet three women and a man, all known only slightly to her. As she went to greet them, it was the man's arm that she took quite naturally, swinging him round to face the Thames as she began to explain the history of the barges on the river.

She dislikes discrimination against women. As Britain's first woman Prime Minister, she has set a record of endurance and success that will take many years, possibly centuries, for another to rival let alone surpass. Though her instinctive preference is for male company, she deeply resents discrimination on grounds of sex. Time and again, she sends back to Whitehall the shortlists of candidates for Government-appointed posts with the demand written in the margin: 'Are there no women who could do this?'

But her dislike of discrimination goes wider than Whitehall's lists of the good and the great. When four of Britain's richest Asians visited her at 10 Downing Street they took with them their wives and seated them at one end of the reception room in anticipation of Margaret Thatcher's arrival. Then the men moved to the other end of the room to be with the Prime Minister when she entered. Whether or not it was part of Asian custom, Margaret Thatcher took in the scene at a glance when she entered. She ignored the men and walked straight over to join the women, where she stayed until the sheepish husbands had no choice but to join her.

One of her greatest pleasures was driving, but it had to end when she became Prime Minister. Her old Vauxhall Viva was pensioned off, and one of her regrets is that because of security she will never be permitted to drive herself again, least of all in an old banger. Her entire future is in a bullet- and bomb-proof Daimler driven by a man trained to handle every crisis that modern-day terrorism can put in his path.

She truly enjoys reading Government papers and relishes

studying long reports, provided they are on key issues. The prospect of having the time at Chequers a few days ahead to read a massive report is said by her aides to be savoured by her in the way that some people look forward to a rich meal. Though she loves absorbing statistics, she dislikes reading in the back of her car and will avoid it whenever possible.

For travel, she prefers the car to the train. Her dislike of riding in trains is in part due to the fact that the railways are nationalised, but also because, for security reasons, the Special Branch insists that an entire carriage is commandeered for her, if not the entire train, and such draconian measures seem unnecessary and undesirable to her. Her dislike of trains on the grounds of nationalisation is not based on ideology so much as on her own personal experience of the inefficiencies of nationalised industries. Since reaching Downing Street she has been persuaded on to a train only twice, and still has vivid recollections of the 1979 train trip to Knutsford, outside Manchester, for a by-election meeting. The train was due to leave Euston at 5.30 p.m. She and her party actually got away at 6.15 p.m. There was no restaurant car, and twenty miles out of Euston the train stopped for two hours.

For total relaxation, Margaret Thatcher enjoys the poems of Rudyard Kipling, a passion which she shares with one of her predecessors, Harold (now Lord) Wilson. She possesses the complete works of Kipling, and likes to quote from them in her speeches. She claims to know all of his poems, but was once caught out by a speech writer, Ronnie (now Sir Ronnie) Millar. 'No,' she said. 'That cannot be Kipling.' She went to the bookshelf to check, and found he was right.

Her favourite piece of Kipling and the poem she quotes most often is 'Runnymede' because, like 'Norman and Saxon', it sums up her feelings about the essential sense of fair play of the British. She will quote it lovingly.

> At Runnymede, at Runnymede!
> Your rights were won at Runnymede:
> No freeman shall be fined or bound,

Or dispossessed of freehold ground,
Except by lawful judgement found
And passed upon him by his peers.
Forget not, after all these years,
The charter signed at Runnymede.

And still when Mob or Monarch lays
Too rude a hand on English ways,
The whisper wakes, the shudder plays
Across the reeds at Runnymede.
And Thames, that knows the mood of kings,
And crowds and priests and suchlike things,
Rolls deep and dreadful as he brings
Their warning down from Runnymede!

She likes to end her quotation of the poem with the words: 'You won't find that in the Labour Party manifesto!'

For relaxing surroundings, she adores the rose garden at Chequers. Sitting there one Sunday she told me: 'This is secure, safe and wonderful.' Something close to bliss for her must be an hour or two spent reading Kipling in the rose garden.

She likes to collect porcelain miniatures, rich Chinese carpets and mementoes of the military, such as the book she was given at Mill Hill Barracks after the Falklands War. The barracks handled all the mail for the military during the conflict, and the Prime Minister was given a book of first issue covers with each page signed by the commanders of every unit that served in the South Atlantic (save for the SAS, who never identify themselves by name). Normally she would hand gifts over to me after receiving them. This one she kept, hugging it to herself, and she carried it back to Downing Street.

She likes everything, whether at work or at home, to be tidy. Asked once in Finchley about her likes and dislikes, she said: 'I've never thought about that.' Then she added: 'I would like everything spick and span. I don't like litter and I like lots of trees.'

Humour is not entirely absent in her character, and she does not positively dislike jokes and wisecracks; but nor does she greatly relish them because, for her, life is too serious a business. Before reaching 10 Downing Street she enjoyed the company of Norman St John Stevas (now Lord St John of Fawsley), who amused her with his wit. But when she became Prime Minister and took him with her into Government, the relationship soon waned as he jokingly dubbed her the 'Blessed Margaret'. An aide said at the time of the sacking of Norman St John Stevas in 1981: 'She found him amusing in the Shadow Cabinet, but not in the real thing.'

Watching Margaret Thatcher at the Grange Farm Estate parties in Finchley, where comic acts are provided for the pensioner guests, is enough to confirm the unhappy way in which she and laughter sit together. She will attempt to feign amusement during the acts (although the humour and fun of the old folk themselves can have her roaring with genuine laughter), but her liking for plain, simple food is not matched by a taste for down-to-earth humour. It sets her face in a heavy, forced smile. As Julian Critchley, the Conservative MP, has remarked: 'Mrs Thatcher is possessed of an armoury of weapons, but humour is not one of them.' Even her enjoyment of the television programmes *Yes Minister* and *Yes Prime Minister*, copies of which were ordered from the BBC so she could watch them at Chequers, stems from the exaggeration of real political life. Her delight comes from inside knowledge enabling her to spot the resemblance between fact and fiction. She is said to have shouted during one episode: 'That's David Howell!'

Situation comedies based on exaggeration of domestic life do not have the same gripping effect on her, and anyone who has glimpsed the Thatchers' household will understand why. She likes home to be a very businesslike place – in some respects an extension of the office. She once said: 'Life doesn't revolve around your home. Home is a base from which you go out to do your own thing.' Because domestic life taken to comic proportions on the television bears little relation to her own idea of domesticity, it therefore does not seem funny. She watches little television compared with the vast majority of people. She has seen *Dallas*, but not

EastEnders. What she dislikes most on the screen, apart from gratu-itous violence, is herself. She has to be coaxed and cajoled to watch her own performances.

She does not like appearing in public with comedians. The most nervous she has been before making a speech was said by Denis Thatcher to have been on the eve of a 'Saints and Sinners' charity lunch where the speakers included comics such as Jimmy Tarbuck. Denis said later that the House of Commons held few terrors for her compared with that occasion. She dislikes the idea that an audience may expect her to make them laugh. Just as comedians and actors are terrified of animals stealing their show, so she is aware that comedians may steal hers.

Since her third General Election victory, she is said by some Ministers to have begun to try her hand at humour. But this observa-tion by Ministers seems to be based more on hope than on experience.

She likes either to meet with a group of two or three people, or to address a crowd of a hundred or more. A figure in between is unwieldy to her and prompts her to take charge. This observation is based entirely on what she says and does in Finchley, but it is a fact that she does not feel at her most comfortable with her 22-strong Cabinet, preferring to work with very small, informal com-mittees of three or four Ministers. She would argue that with three other people it is possible to hold a conversation and discussion, and that with a hundred or more they can be addressed. But something in between and she does not seem to know quite how best to handle them. Consequently, she dominates.

She does not so much like the sound of her own voice, as critics have suggested, as dislike a lull in a conversation or speech. She has a deep and instinctive antipathy to a pause, regarding it almost as an inefficient moment in history which should be filled without further delay. There are no unnatural pauses in conversations with her. If a room or a group falls silent because of her arrival, she will plead: 'Please, why have you stopped talking?' There is no time for a moment's quiet thought with her. She expects everyone to be able, as she is, to think and speak simultaneously. If others cannot, she will do the speaking for them.

In gatherings where she is expected to circulate, she has a particular method of doing so: always in a clockwise direction, and never doubling back on herself. Occasionally, people she has already met will dart ahead to try to speak with her again, only to be asked a question that brooks no answer: 'I've spoken with you before, haven't I?' Headmasters at schools she plans to visit are told by the Special Branch officers who are sent in advance to clear the security hurdles that they will have to change their plans for the tour of the building. She insists on being taken on a route which involves no doubling back. She takes the same approach to travel, regarding any retracing of the journey as a manoeuvre that should always be avoided because it is the product of bad planning and wastes time. On two occasions in six years in Finchley it seemed to me to be impossible to avoid doubling back, so I chose routes through the back streets to try to disguise the manoeuvre. Each time from the back of the Diamler a voice asked with quiet mischief: 'Caught you! We're going back on ourselves and you are trying to hide it, aren't you?'

Margaret Thatcher has favourite dresses (usually blue), and there is also a favourite day for dressing up: the old people's Christmas party at the Grange Farm Estate. For this event she will always wear a full-length dress – once a royal blue one with gold trimmings that seemed more suited for dinner at Buckingham Palace – and always a gown that would not be out of place at a ball. Once, when surprise was expressed at the way she dressed up for the old-age pensioners, she smiled and said: 'But they always expect something glamorous from me.'

She likes to plant trees or inspect guards of honour in a full and proper manner. Both functions are political rituals but she likes to set about them as if the entire day's energy had to be put into the task. Not for her the turning of the first well-sieved sod, with the park keeper planting the tree properly when the dignitaries have gone. Called on to open a conservation project in Finchley, she rolled up her sleeves, set to with the spade and left the mountain ash with the words: 'At least you won't have to plant that again when I'm gone.' She is the same when abroad. In the blazing sun in

[203]

Kenya she was asked to plant a tree, and did so as if she were a twenty-year-old. After a couple of dozen spadefuls of dry Kenyan earth had been rammed into the hole, she stuck her spade in the ground and declared proudly: 'There's a bit of British productivity for you!'

Equally intense when she inspects a guard of honour, she will seek to carry out the inspection while walking – perhaps marching is a better word – in time with the music. The resulting gait would be funny if her eyes were not filled with interest at the passing uniforms. She does not regard the task as a meaningless ritual but, as with everything she does, performs it with exactness.

She likes to talk with old people, particularly in Finchley and the more so if they are Conservative Association members, about the minutiae of their lives and families, displaying an extraordinary memory for detail. But in general, there is no place in her life for light, frothy conversation and the trivial talk of social occasions. Her idea of small talk would probably be an intense discussion on the correct motorway junction by which to leave in order to reach a town in the shortest possible time.

It is not that Margaret Thatcher cannot relax and lighten her spirits. She enjoys a good sing-song at the old people's Christmas party where, with a strong voice, she will join in the renditions of 'Daisy' and other old favourites, often calling loudly for more.

The Prime Minister does like to sleep, contrary to the impression that she enjoys working and living on four hours' sleep a night. At a Number 10 reception after the Moscow Olympics, she overheard a group of athletes talking about her and walked up to ask what they were saying. Daley Thompson, the Olympic gold medallist, said they had heard she got by on just four hours' sleep a night and wanted to know how she managed it. She said: 'Daley, just like you: training and discipline.' In fact, on a Saturday night at Chequers, she looks forward to catching up with nine hours' sleep, after the exertions and trials of a week spent governing a nation.

'If she thinks a Minister is no longer up to it, then he's out.' (Lord Havers, former Lord Chancellor who went 'out' in 1987)

16

THE ACHIEVEMENTS

WHILE THE political colour is wrong, the character comparison of Margaret Thatcher to the Queen of Hearts in Lewis Carroll's *Alice in Wonderland* is uncanny. Her influence over the rest of the Cabinet can be measured by one fact: since she took power on 4 May 1979, all her Cabinet Ministers save three have departed, either voluntarily or involuntarily. In her tenth year in office, the three remaining members of that 1979 team are: Sir Geoffrey Howe, Foreign Secretary and former Chancellor of the Exchequer; Peter Walker, Secretary of State for Wales and former Minister of Agriculture and Energy Secretary; and George Younger, Defence Secretary and former Secretary of State for Scotland.

The roll-call of the banished and vanished serves to underline her own continuity: Francis Pym; Sir Ian Gilmour; Christopher Soames; David Howell; Patrick Jenkin; Viscount Whitelaw; Norman Tebbit; Nicholas Edwards; Mark Carlisle; Baroness Young; Norman St John Stevas; Leon Brittan; Michael Heseltine; Sir Michael Havers; Michael Jopling; John Biffen; Earl Gowrie; John Nott; James Prior; Lord Carrington; Lord Cockfield; Humphrey Atkins. Some wanted to go; others did not. But the list makes one very important point to any Minister entering the Cabinet for the first time: other men and women may come and go, but Margaret Thatcher remains.

With every passing year, and every passing Cabinet Minister, her pre-eminence as the first among equals increases, and the continuing threads of policies running through the Government can be seen more and more as her own. It is the same story on the international scene. She has seen in and out an American President serving the maximum period under that country's constitution. She is also now by far the most senior of the Heads of Government in the twelve-member European Economic Community.

Her single most successful achievement has been the curing of what was known as the 'British disease', the seemingly never-ending decline of the United Kingdom in comparison with its international competitors. This decline was a fruitful source of television documentary material for American film producers, who found new ways to express an old and very sad truth: that until 1979 the British economy had been in decline relative to other advanced countries for over a century. Between 1870 and 1976 output per head in Britain increased less than fourfold while the increase in fifteen other major countries averaged more than sixfold. Since Margaret Thatcher took power, the British annual rate of growth per head in manufacturing has been the highest of the world's seven principal industrial countries.

How has the cure been achieved? Essentially, by the British worker, who is now operating in a deregulated society where the proportion of money taken by the State in taxes is falling. Income tax was slashed in the first nine years of Margaret Thatcher's Government from 33 per cent to 25 per cent, and State spending as a percentage of Gross Domestic Product has fallen from 43.25 per cent in 1979–80 to 41.25 per cent. Put another way, State spending was growing in 1978–9 at a rate of 3 per cent and in 1986–7 at 1 per cent. Economic growth averaged nearly 3 per cent a year over six successive years, and manufacturing output has risen by over 10 per cent since the 1983 General Election.

These achievements are the facts that lie behind the transformation of the British disease into the British economic recovery miracle. American film producers still fly into the United Kingdom to make their documentaries, but now they are all finding new ways to explain this change. In America itself, the political agenda includes discussion of how the 'Thatcher Revolution' can be imported.

Nowhere were the effects of the British disease better illustrated than in strikes. In 1978–9 the industrial disruption reached its nadir with the 'Winter of Discontent'. This was when the trade unions, with whom the Labour Government was supposed to have a 'special relationship', kicked even their own Prime Minister, James Callaghan, as the country went down. Inflamed by inflation and flushed with the power put into their hands by the weak Government, they staged strikes in areas that shocked even the Labour Cabinet. In Liverpool and other major cities, the bereaved could not bury their dead. Hospitals were picketed and cancer patients turned away. Nearly nine and a half million working days were lost.

In no area has Margaret Thatcher's resolve been stronger than in introducing new trade-union laws. The way she handled the problem – as well as successive Employment Secretaries along the way – illustrates something of her approach to major political issues. Her first Employment Secretary, James Prior, who favoured a 'softly-softly' approach with the trade unions, spent the first years of her Government trying to curb her determination to remove special legal immunities from the unions. She allowed herself to be restrained until she judged the general political and public mood to have caught up with her. Then she axed James Prior and brought in right-winger Norman Tebbit to do the job. It has been a similar story in other areas, such as education and health. What happens is that the right wing of her party signals the point of radical change that she wants to reach, the political temperature rises, the public mood begins to change and then any Cabinet Minister not swift enough to respond is replaced by someone with the will to carry through her wishes. She is a mixture of visionary conviction politician and cautious, realistic and pragmatic politician. I believe that Finchley helps her to formulate firm policies from the grass-root gut feelings she first picks up in the constituency. It is her vital link with what the people want, and she is intuitively in tune with it.

The succession of union laws she has introduced each alternate year has led to restrictions on picketing and secondary picketing, compensation for unreasonable exclusion from closed shops, and new rules to ensure that eight out of ten workers must approve a new closed shop in a secret ballot. Union officials have been made liable for damages where they are responsible for unlawful industrial actions, and lawful trade disputes have been restricted to those between workers and their own employers. Secret ballots every five years for union executives have also been introduced. The effect of all this on the strike record of Britain has been dramatic. The number of working days lost through strikes fell from 28,474,000 in 1979 to 6,402,000 in 1985, though the number did bulge in 1984 because of Arthur Scargill's miners' strike, which ended with his ignominious defeat as he sought to defy Margaret Thatcher and her Government.

The deregulation of the economy has brought other major benefits, such as the creation of over a million new jobs between 1983 and 1987, more than in the whole of the rest of the European Community. Because of Margaret Thatcher's tough line on State spending, Britain has become the world's second-largest creditor nation after Japan. Inflation, the evil which she says is never conquered and must always be fought, has been brought down to levels not seen for almost two decades.

The freeing up of the economy has been matched by new freedoms for ordinary people that were once seen as the exclusive privilege and preserve of a certain class of Briton. Over a million families have bought their council homes under the right-to-buy laws. Consequently, the property-owning democracy which is a cornerstone of Margaret Thatcher's political beliefs has increased so that 64 per cent of homes in Britain are now owner-occupied. This compares with 57 per cent in 1979. Since then, 2.5 million more families have become owner-occupiers.

Margaret Thatcher has also turned her ambitions to making Britain a share-owning democracy as well as a property-owning one, arguing that the greater the individual ownership, whether by way of homes or shares, the better for the free-enterprise system. Consequently, under the incentives the Government has introduced, share ownership in Britain has trebled since 1979. Shares are now owned by about 8.5 million people – almost 25 per cent of adults. Employee share schemes, giving workers a slice of profits, increased from just 30 in 1979 to more than 3000 by 1987. Much of the new share ownership is due to the popular sell-offs of major State industries such as British Gas and British Telecom. Instead of handing them to the City or foreign financial institutions to buy, Margaret Thatcher insisted on huge batches of the shares being set aside for small investors. The response surprised even the most optimistic of Ministers.

The effect of privatisation of the State sector was to reduce it by a quarter by 1987. Since then, further sell-offs have been ordered, including the electricity generation and supply industry and the water industry. By February 1987, 600,000 State employees had been transferred to the private sector – and 90 per cent of them had exercised the option of buying shares in their industries. By the 1987 General Election, the revenue raised from these sell-offs had amounted to £4.75 billion and the benefits in increased efficiency were already being seen: British Airways doubled its profits, Jaguar output increased by 8 per cent with 1000 new jobs created, and National Freight increased its profits ninefold.

But perhaps the most startling change of all, and the one of most long-term significance for Britain since 1979, has been in the resurgence of growth of new small firms. It is the growth of these industrial acorns which Margaret Thatcher regards as one of the most important tests of the vitality of an economy. She used to return from visiting President Reagan in the White House in the early years of her Government much troubled and anxious that the birth of massive numbers of new small firms in North America was not being matched on her side of the Atlantic. Now, the boom in new small firms indicates that the British economy has the long-term vibrancy of its North American counterpart. Between 1980 and 1985 there was an average net increase of some 500 new firms every week. In 1987 there were more than 750,000 more self-employed people than in June 1979, making a total of nearly three million, almost 11 per cent of the labour force – the highest for sixty years.

Britain now also employs the smallest Civil Service since the Second World War, down to 599,400 in 1987 – virtually halved compared with what Margaret Thatcher inherited from the Labour Government.

There is a multitude of other successes chalked up during Margaret Thatcher's decade, but they should be measured in ways other than pure statistics. What the Thatcher years have meant for Britain is that the spring has been put back into the step of its people. In the 1970s, the nation believed that decline was inevitable. She has offered back to the British their national pride, along with the freedom to choose. The point about having freedom of choice is that people can still say 'no' and turn back to collectivism and socialism. But the evidence so far would indicate that most people are responding positively to the new choices and freedoms. The result is that Britain as a whole is no longer the poor man of Europe.

For too long, patriotism was a dirty word for the British, but Margaret Thatcher was prepared to say publicly that she is a patriot – and to prove it. She has begun to give the British back their identity, which is something distinct from patriotism. Before she became Prime Minister, she touched briefly on the sensitive subject of national identity when she spoke of the fears of the British of being 'swamped' by immigrants. William (now Viscount) Whitelaw, her erstwhile deputy who was closest to her at that time, reacted against the word and she has never used it since, though her belief has subsequently re-emerged, albeit repackaged in a more sensitive light. During her speech to the General Assembly of the Church of Scotland in May 1988 she said:

People with other faiths and cultures have always been welcomed in our land, assured of equality under the law, of proper respect and of open friendship. There is absolutely nothing incompatible between this and our desire to maintain the essence of our own identity.

[212]

Her belief in the specialness of the British has begun to be transmitted to Britons themselves. If it all sounds a bit simplistic as an interpretation of Margaret Thatcher, then it is an interpretation shared by one of the most complicated of post-war politicians who is also, on many issues, one of her greatest fans: Enoch Powell. He has said that she operates on a relatively limited total of fairly simple ideas and notions: 'She seems to be convinced of what most politicians have ceased to be convinced of, that there are such things as "good guys" and "bad guys", not to say "good" and "evil".'

In a way, Enoch Powell may have come close in his remarks to identifying her greatest achievement of all: that of sharing the simple reactions of ordinary people, who do see most issues in terms of black and white and good and evil. Many intellectuals and academics hate her for it because they have a vested interest in making all aspects of life in general, and politics in particular, appear as complex as possible. Socialists hate her for it because they feel she is stealing votes that by rights should be theirs, often with policies that could be theirs – if their founding constitution did not forbid it. But the people who matter – the British electorate – have repeatedly endorsed the woman and her policies.

Her achievements are based largely, of course, on giving the public broadly what they want. The academics and intellectuals sneeringly describe it as 'populism' and argue that the governance of Britain is really too complicated and important a matter to be dictated by what the British people actually want. They can scoff and sneer as much as they like as far as Margaret Thatcher is concerned. She has not only the political achievements tabulated in the history books, but the economic achievements to match. Call them 'populism', 'Thatcherism' or 'Conservatism', the achievements stand as tall landmarks on the otherwise dreary plains of the post-war years.

She is often asked what is the secret of these achievements. She replies: 'It's really quite simple. What we have done is to re-establish at the heart of British politics a handful of simple truths.' Then she lists the three principal 'simple truths'. First, that the defeat of inflation is always the priority. Second, that people need the incentive that comes from keeping more of what they earn. And third, that as people earn more, they must be allowed to own more, through shares and homes. It really is that simple.

'Bernard Ingham, the bluff Yorkshireman with a volcanic temper, has enjoyed the sort of influence on Margaret Thatcher and on her image that slick advertising men like to pretend they have had.'

17

SPLITTING THE IMAGE

SPLITTING THE image and the image-makers away from the real Margaret Thatcher is difficult, because she was the first British Prime Minister to come to power on the back of a full-scale American-style advertising campaign. Since then, the fact that she has been such a long-serving Prime Minister has to some extent helped to put distance between her and the advertising industry men who were regarded as the 'manufacturers' of Margaret Thatcher – men such as Gordon Reece and Tim Bell, archetypal image-makers, packagers of products and creators of slick one-liners.

After the 1979 General Election, there was a fear within the Conservative Party that both she and it had fallen into the hands of such men – that politics and politicians were being subjugated by the image-makers. The anxieties were understandable although misplaced, and it took until the 1987 General Election for proof to be provided of the baselessness of these fears. In 1979, with Saatchi and Saatchi at their most brilliantly creative on behalf of the Conservative Party, neither the Labour nor Liberal Parties came close to competing in terms of advertising, marketing and media skills. In 1983, the Labour Party positively renounced such skills of the twentieth century, under a leader whose contribution to imagery was to appear at the Cenotaph in Whitehall for the Remembrance Sunday memorial service wearing a donkey jacket.

In 1987 the Labour Party not only caught up with the present-ational and marketing skills of the Conservative Party over the two previous General Elections, but in some respects it exceeded Saatchi and Saatchi in what was to prove their final election campaign for the Conservatives. Labour's party election broadcasts were imaginative and based on clear strategies. Neil and Glenys Kinnock were in touch with ordinary working people, because those were their roots. Neil Kinnock was projected as being proud of Britain, a patriot walking on the cliff top – subliminally the white cliffs of Dover for many people – while a jet fighter roared in the distance above the sea. The nation was thus seeing all the right images (though ironically, no one at the time seemed to notice that the jet fighter was an American F–111 fighter bomber, the type that Margaret Thatcher allowed President Reagan to unleash from American bases in England to bomb Libya and to which Neil Kinnock objected with such hyperbole). But all this image-making did Neil Kinnock and the Labour Party little good. Margaret Thatcher and the Tories still won, after what was not one of her best campaigns, by 101 seats.

The reason for the Labour Party's failure, and one that Neil Kinnock found hard to accept – he refused to believe the opinion polls even at the last moment – is that imagery, advertising and marketing work only if they are projecting genuine strengths of a product or, in the political arena, a set of policies. In the pre-1979 days when Margaret Thatcher was in Opposition, and then during her first election, the reason that the Saatchi and Saatchi team was so successful in positioning her and the Party as representing freedom, opportunity, individual responsibility, choice and prosperity was that under her the Tories themselves were beginning once more to believe in the concepts.

The extent to which the advertising brains helped Margaret Thatcher win in 1979 is a question by which their industry, and especially Saatchi and Saatchi, benefit from seeing it debated. Even to suggest that the advertising industry or a particular advertising agency can be responsible for the winning or losing of a General Election is to endow them with almost mystical qualities that help them gain new business between elections. My own belief is that she would have won even if Saatchi and Saatchi had been working against her, and there can be few better sources of evidence than James Callaghan, the Labour Prime Minister whom she ousted. Before the election he remarked privately to his aides that at times in the course of the history of a nation there is a sea change in the mood of its people. His sense as a politician told him that this was such a time. A handy excuse being prepared by a tired Prime Minister? Hardly. The whole drive of intellectual argument had, at first imperceptibly in the early 1970s, begun to move against socialism and towards the deregulation of the economy. It was the free-thinking right that was producing new arguments, new theories and new proposals. Nor was this taking place merely in the minds of a few economists and politicians. Opinion poll after opinion poll was showing that the nation knew, for instance, that nationalisation had failed. What were needed were new answers to old problems. Mrs Thatcher and Thatcherism arrived to provide those answers.

Of course, men such as Gordon Reece, Tim Bell and others helped to 'soften' her image after she became Opposition Leader and went into the run-up to the 1979 General Election. But this softening appears to have been much more at her instigation than theirs. She is aware – perhaps more so as a woman Prime Minister than most men – just how much she is a 'product' that needs to be marketed and sold. It was not unusual, therefore, for Margaret Thatcher to question, not for the first time, whether she was projecting the right 'personal' image. Comparison of photographs of her taken in 1975 when she became Conservative Party Leader with those taken during and after the 1979 General Election tell the story. She had her teeth capped. She changed her hairstyle, a decision that seems to have been hers alone, to give it a gentler line, removing a certain harshness that had existed beforehand. She moderated her tone of voice too, which was perhaps not so difficult or surprising for someone who had, as a child, gone to elocution lessons. The overall result was a woman who in appearance seemed to have shed years rather than gained them between 1975 and the early 1980s. This self-appraisal was not an isolated occurrence. She repeats the exercise from time to time, as, before the 1987 General Election, she called in an outside adviser to discuss clothes and her image. Again it appears to have been her own decision, though it is one that seems to surprise some men around her. But men generally have a different attitude to clothes and personal presentation.

If her success in 1979 was politically inevitable, as I believe it was, and the advertising men and image-makers were but an adjunct to the surge of a new political and economic philosophy, then their usefulness lay merely in helping to highlight not only the political policies that were suddenly so in tune with the popular mood, but the aspects of Margaret Thatcher that could personalise these policies. Suddenly, it was presentationally useful to have a woman Leader of the Opposition who had a deep hatred of inflation, while the Labour Government was presiding over runaway prices. All she had to do was to behave in public like the housewife she is in private. Similarly, with the soaring bill for public expenditure, she had merely to allude to the housewife's need to budget and she was scoring political points that few men in Britain could hope to achieve. Looking back to the time around 1979, it is possible that the advertising and marketing men were at fault for restraining her too much, for agreeing that her image should be softened. For the subsequent years were to show that much of her appeal is in providing a style of leadership that can at times be abrasive.

What her experience with the advertising men showed was not so much their influence over her as her willingness to learn from them. However, once the door of 10 Downing Street shut behind her on 4 May 1979, they were firmly on the outside. Of course, figures such as Gordon Reece and Tim Bell, the two names most known to the outside world, were still invited back from time to time. But when they did go back, it was only for the occasional social occasion. For behind the door of 10 Downing Street, the Civil Service keeps a jealous hold on the Prime Minister. However, among their number was one man who has perhaps had a real influence on both Margaret Thatcher and her image: Bernard Ingham, the longest-serving Press Secretary at Number 10.

Bernard Ingham, the bluff Yorkshireman with a volcanic temper, has enjoyed the sort of influence on Margaret Thatcher and on her image that slick advertising men like to pretend they have had. Ingham began working for her with an advantage that no one from advertising or the private sector could ever have. By its very nature, the role of Press Secretary at 10 Downing Street is an anonymous one with no public profile and with a huge Civil Service machine in the background into which Ingham could disappear, his pension rights intact, should he fail in his new job. Outside, the marketing men had to ensure either that their agencies were rewarded with occasional publicity or that they were sufficiently well known for their efforts to be able to reap the benefits subsequently. Eventually, Bernard Ingham was to become almost a household name, but the publicity that came his way took many years to arrive and was never sought.

Initially a journalist, an industrial correspondent on *The Guardian*, Ingham had switched to Whitehall and its information service in the heady days of socialism. Indeed, he had once stood as a Labour local government candidate and had served as press chief to Labour's Tony Benn as Secretary of State for Energy, before proletarianism totally overcame the man who had previously been Anthony Wedgwood-Benn and prior to that Lord Stansgate. However, none of Ingham's antecedents was sufficient to persuade Margaret Thatcher to veto him as Whitehall's choice. In fact, extraordinary as it sounds today, she did not see him or interview him before she appointed him. He was the Civil Service's choice with a track record of professionalism, and that was good enough for her. When he arrived at Number 10 from the higher echelons of the Civil Service to which he had been promoted for his administrative skills, she seems to have recognised him as a true professional. He is as sharp an operator in his field as the advertising and marketing men are in theirs. Of course, what he had to handle was the Prime Minister, while they had had only the Leader of the

Opposition to deal with. What, then, did he find in the product he was charged with selling to the nation's press and television?

A good insight to this question came in an unsolicited comment over the luncheon table from one of Bernard Ingham's erstwhile colleagues. He said: 'Of course, it was Bernard Ingham who made Margaret Thatcher what she is. He went out and sold the Prime Minister to the lobby correspondents. But the Prime Minister he sold was not quite the woman she was, at least not at the time he was selling her.'

At that time, in the early months of 1980 and then in the early 1980s themselves, Margaret Thatcher was a rebel in her own Cabinet. It was a Cabinet the majority of whom wanted, by instinct and practice, to run the economy and society in what was for them the old way: the paternalist way of the Whitelaws, Gilmours and Pyms, men who by nature when they came under pressure sought to find the middle ground, the consensus, on any issue. The Prime Minister wanted to march the whole lot over to even older ground, to the philosophy and economics which had lived in the home of her father and which had permeated all her major speeches since she entered Parliament. But she was also very cautious, both as a woman and as a Prime Minister, in making the moves towards her goals. There was no doubt what her targets were. The years since 1979 are littered with speeches that are memorials to her goals, as well as a good few political corpses of Cabinet Ministers who tried once too often to stand in her way. Always cat-like, always long-termist, she was at times almost frozen in those early months in Number 10 between the paralysing forces of a Civil Service and a Cabinet each seeking to impose its will. Together they amounted, too often it seemed to her, to one message: it can't be done.

Margaret Thatcher therefore began the long process of bringing into Number 10 and then into the top posts in Whitehall men and women who would give her a different message: what she was to call the 'can do' message. Bernard Ingham was one of the first of the 'can do' civil servants around her. For all his bluffness, Ingham had sensitively attuned antennae, though at times these do seem to be protruding from a human bulldozer. It did not take his antennae long to pick up precisely what Margaret Thatcher was about as a politician.

He also appears to have made a significant decision very early on in his new career at 10 Downing Street. He was going to be the Press Secretary to the Prime Minister, not to the Government. In the short history of the post, although it has always been Press Secretary to the Prime Minister, in practice its incumbents have regarded themselves as speaking for the Government. To many people there will seem to be no difference: the Prime Minister *is* the Government. Bernard Ingham also took that view, though as an intelligent and experienced operator on the inside of Whitehall he knew better than most people that there is a crucial distinction. A Press Secretary to the Prime Minister leads with his chin. A Press Secretary who is looking to the Government will wait for the rest of the Cabinet to catch up with what the Prime Minister is saying in private, lest the view of the Government as a whole does not coincide with that of the Prime Minister.

It therefore followed that at crucial early points in the life of the Government, such as in the run-up to public spending rounds, Budgets, strikes and the like, Bernard Ingham would lead with his chin on behalf of the Prime Minister. Every weekday morning he would meet with her for fifteen minutes to discuss what he believed the media would want to know and how to handle it. With Ingham clearly representing the views of the Prime Minister and speaking entirely non-attributably to the lobby correspondents for transmission in the newspapers and over the air waves, the line of communication could clearly in theory avoid the Cabinet.

Of course, it could be argued that Margaret Thatcher herself saw the advantages of using Bernard Ingham as a by-pass to the Cabinet in those vital early years, but there is no doubt in Whitehall that this was not in fact the case. As a novice Prime Minister she needed all the support she could secure as she sought to handle both the Cabinet and the Civil Service machine. It is important to remember the political atmosphere of those days. Margaret Thatcher was seeking to blaze her new economic trail in the face of an unexpected massive hike in the price of oil that was plunging the world into recession. Many of her own Conservative back-benchers thought she would be ditched before the next General Election, and the opinion polls were plunging for the Tories in general and for her in particular.

What Bernard Ingham saw was a threatened but very determined woman with a vision. The Yorkshireman did on the national political canvas what this down-to-earth Glaswegian sought to do in Finchley when the going got rough. He picked up her vision and, on her behalf, he ran with it. In private she was at times cautious, hesitant and uncertain. So instead of waiting to see whether other Ministers would be able to capitalise on her weaknesses, Ingham took the essence of Margaret Thatcher out to the media. He scoffed at the idea of U-turns. He disparaged faint-hearts in the Cabinet. A crisis over proposals to cut planned rises in Government spending? Ministers would just have to find the cuts or she would sort them out. Listening to Ingham gave the media the certain impression that there was a ferocious tigress on the loose in Whitehall. The image seemed to shriek that if anyone unwarily crossed her path, she would kill as soon as look at them.

The reality was very different. In those early years, she con-structed and reconstructed her Cabinet with immense caution. It was not until she had been in office for three years that she began to operate fully in accordance with the image.

Whether the public believed even half of Bernard Ingham's outpourings as transmitted to them via the lobby system, it did not really matter. Probably, most people did not. The nation had been conditioned to a diet of political expediency, of U-turns and economic stops and starts. The underlying mood was one of mild cynicism and the general public expectation was that she would probably go the same way as her predecessors. However, in those early days Bernard Ingham wanted to make a point as much to the Civil Service, Ministers and Margaret Thatcher herself as to the nation at large. He gave the Prime Minister much-needed confi-dence through his unattributable activities and the fruits they bore in the newspapers; and his covert activities also struck fear into the very hearts of both civil servants and Ministers, who read the political content of newspapers more assiduously than most of the electorate.

The attitude that politicians take towards the press is best summed up by a former political correspondent who went on to work for Conservative politicians. He said that a constant question put to him by various MPs and Ministers involved the sources of stories that appeared in the newspapers. He said: 'Sometimes I would say, often because I had not the remotest idea where the story had come from, "Oh, he [the writer] probably made it up." Not once did a politician so much as half-believe me, and the point of the story is not one about journalists but to illustrate the fact that every politician believes that every item that appears in news-papers has as its origin another politician, who got it there with a particular purpose in mind.' In the case of Bernard Ingham, he did have one overall purpose: to underpin the authority and vision of Margaret Thatcher. In Whitehall and among Ministers, his strong message through the media began to spread fear. For no civil servant likes to lose a Minister, and the merest implication that a Minister is under some form of threat from the Prime Minister will have a disproportionate impact on the efforts of the civil servants.

In short, Bernard Ingham waged a propaganda war on Whitehall itself and in the process rapidly gave Margaret Thatcher the confi-dence she needed to play the role he was projecting. Not for nothing was he subsequently to be dubbed by sections of the Press as the 'Deputy Prime Minister'. Not for nothing has he been known to dress down junior Ministers – to their faces, not third-hand through the media. And not for nothing has the demise of three senior Cabinet Ministers – one in each Parliament – been laid in part at his door.

It was not simply a question of Ingham creating a role and image for the Prime Minister which she then adopted. He simply gave a firm outline of the role and painted in the image before she got there herself in the course of her own natural development as Prime Minister. Inevitably, the role and image that he projected and which stuck with the world were cruder than the reality. By the very nature of the work he was doing, the complexities and shades of the Prime Minister could not be portrayed. But if he had held back and lagged behind her – let alone behind her Government – then her early days in 10 Downing Street would have been even more hazardous than they were.

Ingham has learned to read her mind. He does not need detailed briefings from her or other Downing Street officials. Hand him a pile of Government papers outlining the problem and setting down a series of choices of action and Ingham will know almost as quickly as the Prime Minister what decision to take. Both colleagues and observers say he has become telepathic.

The relationship has deepened into one of total trust and loyalty. She has an unwavering faith in his judgement on media matters and presentation. He puts great store by loyalty to her. When his wife was critically injured by a runaway lorry during the Falklands crisis in 1982, he insisted on dashing back and forth between hospital and Number 10. Her loyalty to him is equally fierce – and well founded. She could do with more like him around her.

'Even before the 1983 General Election, Norman Tebbit said that she would go on to become to politics what Queen Victoria was to the monarchy'.

18

HOW HISTORY WILL SEE HER

In the Members' Lobby at the Commons, through which MPs walk to and from the chamber, there are statues of great Parliamentarians of earlier years, including Winston Churchill, Clement Attlee and Lloyd George. There is also an empty plinth, and one day there will be a statue of Margaret Thatcher on it. She would have been entitled to the honour simply by virtue of the fact that she was Britain's first woman Prime Minister. She is now entitled to it not because of her sex, but because of her achievement. No other Prime Minister this century can equal her record for length of service. The decision to erect the statue will in all probability be taken when she has left the Commons; four or five years ago the very proposal, which needs cross-party support in the Commons, would have been blocked by many Labour MPs.

Today, even some Labour MPs would agree with the assessment by Lord Hailsham, Lord Chancellor in the first eight years of Margaret Thatcher's Government, that she has to be put in the same category as queens of earlier centuries. Love her or hate her, the record stands and even her most ferocious socialist opponent will admit to admiration of the sheer perseverance that has taken one woman through three General Elections and Britain through an economic and now a social revolution.

There has been another, and this time cross-party change of attitude over the last four or five years of her Premiership, which can be illustrated by the words of two Tory MPs, one speaking before, and the other after, this change had occurred. The first marched across the Members' Lobby in Margaret Thatcher's first Parliament telling everyone who would listen to him: 'It will be fifty years before this country has another woman Prime Minister – from any party.' He found few MPs across the parties who were inclined to disagree with this view. The second remark was heard some six years later after her third election victory when a group of right-wing Conservative MPs were chatting at a celebration reception at Conservative Central Office in London. They were thoughtfully discussing who the next Leader of the Conservative Party might be – a regular topic of conversation at Westminster. After a long pause, one of the MPs said: 'Oh well, I suppose we will just have to hang on for Edwina Currie.' The rest of this right-wing group gazed into their champagne glasses and no one demurred. The important point of the MPs discussion was that the idea of another woman as Party Leader was so obviously unremarkable.

One of the key and unasked questions of the last ten years is whether Margaret Thatcher would have secured all her achievements if she had been a man. It is a question that cannot be answered, but simply posing it is enough to illuminate some of the strengths she has brought to the role.

She took over the Party Leadership in 1975 at a time when Britain, under a Labour Government, was undergoing what most foreign observers, and many domestic ones, saw as the terminal stages of economic, industrial and social decline. Inflation was rampant, the Labour Government was daily ceding power to the union barons, and industrial and social anarchy was reaching its zenith in the 'Winter of Discontent' in 1978. Her faith in the British people has now been vindicated, but the long-termism of her approach to the task of renewing Britain, her resolve and fortitude and at times sheer bloody-mindedness may owe something to the fact that she is a woman.

She certainly believes that her success is helped by her womanhood. In 1975, the year she became Conservative Party Leader, she said: 'In politics, if you want anything said, ask a man. If you want anything done, ask a woman.' Even earlier, at the Conservative Party Conference in Brighton in 1969, ten years before becoming Prime Minister, she addressed a Conference fringe meeting on the subject of women's rights. She concluded with a quotation from Sophocles: 'Once a woman is made equal to a man, she becomes his superior.' Later, after securing the Leadership of the Party, she remarked: 'I owe nothing to Women's Lib. I had balanced myself out and got part of the way there before Lib even started.'

It is women who carry the generation-to-be and who generally have primary responsibility for the next sixteen or so years for bringing them up. Women therefore tend to take the long-term view and then stick to it. This is what evolution has programmed them for, but possibly what most men overlooked when Margaret Thatcher got to Number 10. She was biologically and psychologically geared to rear and mould offspring for a number of years. The fact that after about ten years in office she is showing no sign of immediate retirement should therefore not be too surprising. It may be that, for her, the charge she took on in 1979 is just about to leave primary school. Another five or so years and perhaps she will be ready to cut the apron strings.

As a matter of historical interest, she would need to stay in office until 14 March in the year 2000 to become the longest-serving Prime Minister ever. She would then pass the record of Sir Robert Walpole who served for 20 years 314 days between 3 April 1721 and 11 February 1742. Of course, he had the advantage that in those days it was unnecessary to secure popular support because the idea of one man, one vote was not even a dream – to say nothing of one woman, one vote.

It may be not without significance that since the 1987 General Election she has shown a sharp interest in the year 2000. In the summer of 1988 she invited to Number 10 the editors of Britain's major women's magazines. After lunch she surprised her guests

[231]

with a challenge: to inspire their readers to take part in creating an imaginative and appropriate landmark to commemorate the millenium. She also spoke in Finchley of the ability of Ronald Reagan to hold the office of President of the United States aged seventy-six, and has held this out as an example worth following. Even before the 1983 General Election, Norman Tebbit was saying while he was Trade and Industry Secretary that she would go on to become to politics what Queen Victoria was to the monarchy. At the time, no one took him seriously. Later, after her 1987 General Election win, he commented: 'I think she can go on for a long time and, anyway, what would she do if she wasn't being Prime Minister? Can't imagine her making marmalade for the WI or knitting woollies for the grandchildren. She's a very, very active woman.'

The whole area of the womanhood of British Prime Ministers is as yet unexplored, simply because there is only one by which to judge. But women leaders do seem to be different in the way they manage those around them. For instance, Norman Tebbit observed that women leaders are not 'clubbable'. They are not as prone as men to having a bunch of cronies around them who are relied on for the crucial advice of the day. A woman who has worked closely with Margaret over recent years said that the Prime Minister 'uses people so that she takes the strength from this one and calls on a talent from that one, and so on. She does not have people as such whom she calls on for advice and help.' This might help to explain why she has endured the loss of long-serving members of the Cabinet with less impact on her and her Government than most observers expected.

In the early years at Number 10, male Cabinet colleagues privately predicted that she would 'burn out' or 'blow up'. The pressures and responsibilities of modern-day leadership in Downing Street are immense, greater than ever before in the history of the post. The confident belief that she was supercharged by flows of adrenalin that would one day simply stop, to result in her 'dissolving before our very eyes' as one Conservative MP put it, was echoed by a male civil servant who worked with her at

Number 10. 'One day she will stop and then she'll crumble,' he forecast in 1983. Clearly, the forecast was wrong.

If Margaret Thatcher's strengths as a woman are one reason for her success, then it is perhaps no surprise that she looks to a woman as her idol: Anna Leonowens, of *Anna and the King of Siam*. She was asked at a Savoy lunch in 1960, when she was one of the six Women of the Year, to confess her secret dream of who she would like to be if she were not Margaret Thatcher. She chose Anna Leonowens and explained that she had had 'a sense of purpose and the perseverance to carry out this purpose'. Armed with these, Anna Leonowens had gone to Siam and, because of her, slavery had been abolished there. (It has subsequently been pointed out that she must have been reading Anna Leonowens' self-flattering account of her time in Siam, which was not entirely accurate either about her achievements or about the King of Siam.)

The passage of the years since 1979 and the laying to rest by Margaret Thatcher of the expectation that she would finally slide into U-turns have begun to reveal a figure whom history may judge to be something of a latter-day Victorian nanny. With a firm view of how she wanted her charge to act when it left her care, and certain that the child secretly desired firm discipline, she settled down to the task with the determination and patience of someone who wants to do nothing else for the rest of her life. As a nation we began to lose our way after the First World War, and began the drift to the 'Nanny State'. It took just one nanny in Number 10 to halt the decline and give back to the people a sense of what it feels like to stand on their own two feet.

She believes that she has changed the course of politics in Britain for at least a generation, possibly longer. The other parties are, as she so delicately put it, 'tiptoeing' on to her ground – as are the socialist governments of some foreign countries. This 'tiptoeing' is creating what her former mentor Sir Keith Joseph once described as the 'common ground' – an expression she has used subsequently to describe the ground upon which she believes political parties in Great Britain should fight, and eventually will fight. It is a very narrow strip of political ground on which most issues are taken as common to both warring sides. Competition and a free-enterprise society are seen as the most efficient and morally justifiable ways to run an economy. The role of the State is to be the minimum possible. Every man and woman should have an equal opportunity to rise or fall. Taxation should be the lowest possible consistent with the external and internal defence of the nation. When Sir Keith used the phrase the 'common ground' not long after Margaret Thatcher became Prime Minister it was, as is so much of what he says, totally misunderstood. He used the description too early in the Thatcher years, and the media at large and the simplistic political commentators in general assumed that he was speaking of some sort of consensus in British politics. He was talking of no such thing. What he meant by the 'common ground' was precisely what Margaret Thatcher means today: the basic premises of other parties' arguments shifting towards her beliefs so that they fight like the Republicans and Democrats in the United States of America – with the flag in the corner of each room and a common belief in free enterprise as the best way to create wealth, improve the living conditions of all people and safeguard individual freedom.

Certain political problems remain so long as she is in Number 10 and her successor is unidentified. The problems are, unusually in post-Second World War history, ones of national success rather than national failure. What should Britain's role be within the European Community? Should Britain be part of a common European government? We all know the derisive responses of Margaret Thatcher to such questions. She feels that the instinct of the nation does not yet support even the asking of such questions, let alone the answers of a common European government and a common European currency that some Euro-supporters want to provide.

If political leaders are remembered for their achievements, then Edward Heath's statue at Westminster will be there because he was the leader who took Great Britain into the European Community. Margaret Thatcher's place is guaranteed for her endurance and breaking of Downing Street records, for reversing industrial and economic decline that had become endemic, and for winning a small war on the other side of the world that military historians doubted, on the precedents of length of lines of supply, was possible. She may yet be remembered, too, for preserving Great Britain's independence within the European Community.

But how decisive a turning point in Britain's economic and industrial history will historians see her years in 10 Downing Street as representing? She has changed Britain's economic and industrial performance and begun to change its society and morality. But opinion is divided among even her most ardent right-wing supporters as to whether the change is permanent, whether the 'wrong' Conservative successor could wreck it all, albeit inadvertently, and whether history will judge that the revival was just a blip in the downward slide of a post-imperial nation.

She is reticent on the issue of a successor and how he or she will underpin or undermine her achievements. What we do know is that she believes that a successor is there today in her Government, though not necessarily in her Cabinet. She also believes that the next Leader will need to be different to her in some ways. Perhaps 'not quite so combative as me', she has said, because by the time her successor takes over she will not only have turned round the ship of State but it will be sailing firmly on its new course.

Whoever succeeds her as Conservative Party Leader and, it is to be hoped, as Prime Minister, should have the same essential and instinctive qualities that Margaret Thatcher possesses. By that time, the Cabinet will have within it many 'born-again' Thatcherites – those who now espouse the values she stands for but did not do so as younger men and women when Edward Heath was Prime Minister. It would be invidious to name names, but in the heat of the political kitchen at 10 Downing Street, politicians revert to type and there are still very many in the Party who are not her type but pretend to be so because they see it as the route to power. So when the time comes for a successor, the Conservative MPs in whose hands the choice lies will be deciding not just on an individual but on the place in history of Margaret Thatcher. She may have brought out the best in the British character since 1979, but in the march of British political history she could still be an aberration and so, too, could be the gains that the United Kingdom has secured since then.

When she went into 10 Downing Street on 4 May 1979, she did so quoting the words of St Francis of Assisi:

> Where there is discord, may we bring harmony.
> Where there is error, may we bring truth.
> Where there is doubt, may we bring faith.
> Where there is despair, may we bring hope.

In the months and years that followed, these words were thrown back in her teeth. Unemployment rose and rose, riots broke out throughout the land and she was accused of deliberately turning divisions in society into chasms. The words of St Francis seemed to become more ironic on her lips as the television news film was replayed.

What should be known more widely is the background to her speaking the words on the step of Number 10. She had asked one of her speech writers, Ronnie Millar, to give her some ideas of what she should say on that famous morning before she stepped through that celebrated doorway. When he produced the words of St Francis, she showed her emotion. I have never doubted her desire to secure St Francis's targets; but she was never going to give so much as a moment's thought to trying to secure them other than through her own policies. Since then, as she has staked out a new common ground from which Britons live and work, those words have perhaps begun to be a little better understood by the people of the United Kingdom, and her sincerity acknowledged. For she is an absolutist. The harmony, truth, faith and hope which she sought were not to be achieved swiftly, and they would not have lasted for long at the price of compromise and consensus.

'She has always been so busy, busy, busy that it is difficult not to watch her and wonder whether and how she could live with herself if fate washed her up alone on a desert island.'

19

MARGARET THATCHER AND ME

MARGARET THATCHER once asked: 'Why do all the difficult decisions come to me?' It was a rhetorical question, but asked with something of a weary sigh shortly after she told President Reagan that he could fly his F–111 jets from Britain to bomb Colonel Gadaffi's Libya. Of course, all the difficult decisions go to her because that is what the job of Prime Minister is about. But at that moment, as at others, she seemed to be reflecting not just the loneliness of power but an inner, personal loneliness as well.

It is a personal loneliness that can find her ill at ease with her own company when the despatch boxes are completed, the twins are out of touch, Denis is abroad on business and she faces a Sunday on her own at Chequers. It is then, with twenty-four hours to spare and a gap beginning to yawn in her diary, that at her insistence nine of the key figures from her Conservative Association in Finchley will be phoned, as they were a few weeks after the 1987 General Election, and invited at only a few hours' notice to Sunday lunch at Chequers. She simply had nothing to do, and wanted her friends around her. It is the inner loneliness of a woman who, as she does when she goes off to the West Country for a week's annual holiday in the summer, is compelled after the first day to ask the skeleton staff from Downing Street drafted along with her

[239]

to compile a daily programme of events for her. She has always been so busy, busy, busy that it is difficult not to watch her and wonder whether and how she could live with herself if fate washed her up alone on a desert island.

Busy as she is – and busy as she makes herself – she cannot fill every waking moment of every day with activity. When I worked for her, I found it difficult not to ask myself if, when she does stop, she is happy with just her own idle thoughts. The answer, I suspect, is that there is always a restlessness within her that forever keeps from her the moments of pleasure that so many people find in simply doing nothing.

This half-sensed personal as well as political loneliness of Margaret Thatcher has an important impact on the feelings of those who work closely with her. They become, as I did, intensely protective in a way that goes well beyond that of most officials for their political boss. Combine that essential personal isolation with the loneliness of power, and add to it the fact that she is a woman leader, and perhaps it begins to be understandable that she brings out such protectiveness in those around her.

It is difficult not to notice that she seems to have few friends. Of course, there are Crawfie and Joy in 10 Downing Street, as well as long-standing associates from the Finchley Conservative Association, but there are precious few others who are not politicians of one sort or another. And friendship between politicians is unusual and difficult; those who kid themselves that they have friendships in Westminster are usually confusing friendships with alliances.

For example, Margaret and Denis Thatcher have 'private' drinks parties at Number 10 on the days of the royal garden parties, events that are strictly ruled off by the Civil Service as being of a personal nature and thus paid for by the Thatchers. But the faces of those present are invariably those of politicians, interspersed perhaps with personalities from the world of entertainment who would be on many 10 Downing Street invitation lists regardless of the occupant.

As I worked with Margaret Thatcher, the image of the woman changed in some ways. She was as tough, single-minded and hard-working as she had seemed before. But there is also great compassion and caring in her. Despite her great personal charity and compassion, however, it did seem to me at times that, perhaps because she is such a remarkable and talented woman herself, she found it difficult to appreciate fully the problems of those who are unremarkable: the ordinary folk with too many children, nowhere near enough money and precious little hope. But is it necessary to understand fully their problems and the apparent hopelessness of their lives in order to be best placed to help them? A rising standard of living and maximum freedom of choice are of more practical help than economic stagnation and dependence on the State – no matter how much the latter provides a collectivist shoulder to cry on.

I do not pretend that my six years working with Margaret Thatcher produced a special kinship between us. Our relationship was always very businesslike rather than personal, though it could also at times be warm and close. During the years I worked with her, she revealed many different sides to her character – aspects that are never or scarcely seen by the world at large. She is far too complicated to be summed up in a sentence – or even a book. However, perhaps one final story involving both of us shows her as a good and caring friend.

I had a personal problem and the time came when I felt it should be discussed with Margaret. The conversation, which lasted an hour, proved that this was a woman who could listen, advise and help. But there was one piece of advice that will stay with me, and she gave it both as a woman and a Prime Minister. She urged that whatever decision I took it should not be taken with her in mind. So often, she said wearily, both her friends and members of her family had felt they had to take courses of action which they would not have needed to take were she not Prime Minister. Suddenly my own problem had a different perspective. Clearly, at one level she yearned to be ordinary with an ordinary family and ordinary friends with whom problems could be ordinarily discussed. But try as she might, those around her felt they had to change their lives because she was Prime Minister.

[241]

For me, the most surprising change in my appreciation of Margaret Thatcher was in the way I saw myself. Those who are close to her want to work hard and well, to excel for her sake, and from there it is but a short step to a further intensifying of the fierce loyalty that she brings out in those around her. Having worked for her, I know why soldiers will race up a beach under crackling gunfire behind a captain who has decided to lead right from the front: his men are not so much following the man as trying to get up the beach first to protect him. It's like that working for Margaret.

My experience is not isolated. During the Falklands War, a very senior military officer who was subsequently honoured was required to work every day during the campaign with the Prime Minister. He was not a Thatcherite, not even a Conservative by inclination. He was more middle of the road in his political beliefs, at the time probably favouring Dr David Owen. By the end of the campaign he was one of Margaret Thatcher's greatest fans, and he told friends at the Ministry of Defence that he now understood how the men who had served directly under Lord Mountbatten had felt about their leader.

Once, it was acceptable and even fashionable simply to criticise Margaret Thatcher outright. Now, because of her tenure in office, most people feel it necessary to preface their remarks by saying what a wonderful woman she is before launching into their criticism, which so often stems from their desire to have a Prime Minister who listens to special pleading. At such times the old loyalty wells up again and I find myself ferociously voicing her arguments against governing Britain with special interests in mind. She believes the overriding national interest to be the priority, rather than a lot of minority ones.

Even today, Margaret Thatcher seems to me to be totally misunderstood by much of the nation, even by those who have voted for the Conservative Party and for her in three successive General Elections. Many voted out of self-interest – and there is nothing wrong in that. But what they do not understand is just how much she is driven by a view of the national interest that requires that at one time or another all the special pleaders must have their corns trodden on by Government.

Just as Adam Smith saw the unstoppable 'hidden hand' of market forces, made up of millions of individual decisions, so she believes there is a hidden hand of political will in Britain that, left unfettered, will make Britain once more competitive, prosperous and free. It's a formula that convinced the electorate at one General Election and has been judged by them to be working satisfactorily at two successive ones. Working with a woman who believed in the formula long before the voters had the chance to prove it is an enervating experience. You quickly come to feel that her faith in the British cannot be misplaced.

Working with her it is difficult, too, not to learn and feel something about serving others. The word 'service' today means for most people the speed with which a waiter or shop assistant arrives. Margaret Thatcher was brought up to believe that she had a duty to serve others, as her father served the people of Grantham. Of course, I never knew Alderman Roberts. In fact he died in 1970, just a few months before his daughter went into Government for the first time. But you cannot work for Margaret Thatcher for long without feeling that somehow you did know something of this man who was the model for her life and politics.

What also became clearer as I worked for her is that she has great courage. I am not talking so much of physical courage, though it takes a bit of that in these seemingly ever more dangerous times to remain as Prime Minister. What I am talking about is moral courage. It is this which has kept her standing by her beliefs since they came under public and Parliamentary scrutiny in 1975 when she became Party Leader.

What I see in her now is no more than that which was seen by others who worked with her before she was Prime Minister. During my time with her I came across a statement by Airey Neave, made not long before he was assassinated and just six weeks before she won her first General Election. I realised that his assessment of her then would have scarcely registered on my mind before my years with her, but now it seems almost faultless. From his knowledge of her as a political colleague and personal friend, he summed her up in these words, upon which I cannot improve.

> Although she is serious by nature and as a great patriot is very concerned about the future of this country, there is a humorous side to her and off duty she can be very amusing and has the ability to laugh at herself.
>
> She is self-critical, likes accuracy, enjoys a well-reasoned argument and respects people who know their facts – she has immense powers of concentration and a quite exceptional memory. Her court experience has undoubtedly helped to make her a formidable cross-examiner and she always has her case well prepared.

Then, asked to choose her single predominant characteristic, he replied with prescience:

> I would choose her great personal courage. It may be that she has many frightening experiences to come but the thing she will never lack is courage. That is her great quality. She is outspoken by nature and is essentially a fighter, and nobody should be surprised if she tells the country a few home truths.

The IRA took Airey Neave's life before she began to fulfil in Downing Street a description of her that was to prove so accurate as to be uncanny.

I would add just one rider to Airey Neave's brilliant summary. I do so because there is an unease that bothers me from time to time as I reflect on my years working for her and the Party. It stems from the fact that there is something not quite right after a decade in Number 10 about many of the Ministers whom she has appointed and promoted. She sometimes seems to me to be too attracted by those who have been to public school and who come from political, wealthy or landed families. They all act according to her will now, and behave as born-again Thatcherites. But anyone who shares both her beliefs and her background, and who has watched the rise and rise of those who do not share her convictions, cannot be anything but uneasy. At times she senses this herself, but seems happy to be a prisoner of the Government Whips' Office and to accept its recommendations for junior appointments – who subsequently become middle-ranking Ministers and who are then those from whom she must choose to fill Cabinet vacancies.

This system of appointments through, from and via the Whips' Office, whose incumbents in turn recommend who should succeed them when they move into Ministries, leaves a Prime Minister with less personal choice than most outsiders imagine. Am I suggesting a conspiracy? Not quite. For Margaret Thatcher seems to be condoning what might otherwise amount to a conspiracy by her over-willingness to accept the Eton-educated offspring of the Party grandees and paternalists. Nor am I suggesting that she is a snob, a claim that has been made by some who knew her at Oxford. Instead, I suspect that the imbalance among those Ministers who are now around her arises largely because she is too trusting. She could well do with being a little more suspicious, especially with some of those in the self-perpetuating Government Whips' Office.

The paternalistic side of the Party did not simply throw in the towel when Margaret Thatcher won her second General Election, and anyone who doubts it should look at the hard political facts in the House of Commons and the Government today. The Party in the Commons can muster at least a hundred MPs who are conviction Thatcherites. Yet if Margaret Thatcher stepped down from power, these hundred MPs would have difficulty in finding a potential candidate. If this sounds rather too gloomy a note upon which to end, then it is merely because I am – and was during my years with Margaret – the most impatient and enthusiastic of her converts.

I find some reassurance from those MPs on the right of the Party who argue that Margaret Thatcher has secured such a revolution since 1979 that the axis of politics could never slip back, that the new centre ground is here to stay. But I do not find total reassurance in what these MPs say. For I recollect how Edward Heath was once 'Selsdon Man', a new right-winger with policies to match after the Shadow Cabinet met at the Selsdon Hotel in Surrey, prior to the 1970 General Election, and drew up a draft manifesto. But the heat and pressure of being in Number 10 always reveals the very heart of the politician, and when the going got hot and rough for Edward Heath, he melted. Recalling what Heath achieved in his four years should be warning enough of just how little time would be needed to undo so many of the achievements of the last ten should the succession fall into the wrong hands.

My belief in a Thatcherite future springs not so much from the Conservative Government as it is constructed today, not so much from the belief of right-wingers that the axis of politics has been irreversibly changed, as from the revolution taking place in the Conservative Associations themselves. It is a revolution so deep within the individual Associations and with such far-reaching consequences that I doubt today if Margaret Thatcher herself recognises its enormity. As her former agent who maintains a close contact with what is going on in Associations in Scotland, England and Wales, I may, just for once, have even more of an insight into the matter than she has. This revolution, if successful, guarantees a truly Thatcherite Party and Government in the 1990s if she continues at the head of the Party and in Number 10 through the next General Election and the one after – as I hope she will.

It could well be that Margaret Thatcher's timetable for eventual departure will be determined by the arrival at Westminster of this new generation of Thatcherite MPs. They will be at hand to support her at the next General Election and the one after that. There is no doubt that a huge wave of them is coming. In England, Wales and Scotland the Associations are picking prospective Conservative Parliamentary candidates who reflect the constituencies. In Scotland today, the Laird is not automatically granted an interview when a place falls vacant for a Conservative candidate. In England, the landed gentry and the sons of former Conservative MPs receive scarcely more favoured treatment. The son of a former MP or Cabinet Minister may secure an interview with a Conservative Association but today he or she will not get to the last three in the final selection except on merit.

Out in the country at large the Thatcherite revolution is fuelled by the former council tenants who now own their homes and probably a small portfolio of shares as well. It is these men and women who now not only have a voice and a vote in the running of their children's schools but also belong to their local Conservative Associations and are determining who will be the prospective Conservative candidates. It is this new wave of Thatcherite MPs who will help determine her successor.

I find this revolution tremendously exciting, not least because it is bringing to fruition the dreams that I nurtured as a Young Conservative forty years ago in Glasgow. It spells the beginning of the end for the Conservative Party of the grandees and pater-nalists, strong though they may still be today in some quarters of the Conservative Party at Westminster. Ten years ago, many of them were content enough to come to power on Margaret Thatcher's slogan of 'Power to the people'. Today they are begin-ning to realise that they must pay the price. That price will be an army of men and women at Westminster who share the same values as Margaret Thatcher and who are already on the road there.

If I am right and she intends to go on in Number 10 long beyond her first ten years, then she and this army of Thatcherite Conser-vative MPs will be on their way to overturning two of the oldest laws of politics. First, that great leaders pay scant attention to providing the right successor. Second, that all political power ends in sadness. It would be fitting if a woman who has achieved so much that seemed impossible was able, finally, to turn even those two laws on their head.